I Dare Ya!

Secrets to Successfully Attracting and Retaining Jewish Audiences

Pamela Richards Saeks

Book and Cover design by Be Bold Creative.

For information contact:

Be Bold Creative
www.beboldcreative.net

Ellipsis Publishing
P.O. Box 62609
Cincinnati, OH 45262

ISBN: 978-0-578-58217-7

First Edition: October 2019

Printed in the United States of America

10 9 8 7 6 5 4 3 2 1

This book is dedicated to my lifelong partner,

Change.
Thank you for continuing to push me.
I will never stop pushing for you.
Your faithful agent, P.

And…

To my other lifelong partner and husband,
Sonny.
Your love and support keep me going!

And… my business partner,
Trevor,
For sticking by my side through thick and thin.

Author's Notes

The case studies and examples cited in this book are fictionalized versions of actual, real-world situations that I've encountered over the course of my career.

A special note to all data and grammar wonks who will undoubtably judge me when they see the phrase, "data talks." I know the word is plural and it should be "data talk" or "datum talks"... but seriously - no one actually "talks" that way so please save your red pen for more important mistakes you're sure to find such as typos, missing periods, misuse of semicolons, overuse of exclamation points and more.

Out of respect to all readers, I have chosen to hyphenate the word G-d throughout this book.

Contents

Warning!

This book takes an honest and unapologetic approach to helping you successfully attract your target audience and keep them coming back... even if it means breaking the rules.

What I'm going to tell you works... but only if you're willing to cast aside your ego, get out of your comfort zone and prepare to persuade the powers that be to get with the program, because here's the deal --

Change is hard.

Change is scary.

Change threatens the status quo.

And it's going to take courage and commitment, and a certain amount of good old-fashioned chutzpah to pull it off. Do you have what it takes?

Okay, good! Read on -- ***but be warned...***

I won't be walking on eggshells, nor will I waste your time

sugar-coating the truth, or only telling you what you want to hear. If that's what you're after, head to the nearest Jewish mother where you're sure to get all the unconditional love and approval you need.

But if you're bold enough to take a good hard look in the mirror, and if you're willing to do what it takes to make real change...

Get ready...

Get set...

Let's go...

I Dare Ya!

In the Beginning...

"...And G-d said, 'let there be light,' and there was light."

If only we, as mere mortals, could just snap our fingers and create miracles. If only we could so effortlessly shed light on one of the most confounding mysteries of our age: **How to effect transformative change** – because, few things are quite as difficult.

And while we didn't get the G-d-given gift of being able to turn infinite darkness into light, we did get a pretty great set of rules for how to live our lives, which has held up amazingly well for thousands of years. So, taking that as inspiration, I decided to come up with my own set of guidelines for successfully engaging people in Jewish life...

- Because so many congregations and Jewish organizations across the country are experiencing a steep decline in membership and participation.

- Because competition for people's time and attention is fiercer than ever before.
- And because so many of those people say that traditional ways of "being" and "doing Jewish" lacks meaning and relevance in their lives.

That's the reason I've devoted most of my life to cracking the code - to figuring out new and better ways to engage Jewish people who feel disaffected and estranged - to bring them back in, or engage them for the first time, and keep them coming back for a lifetime...

...Here's what I believe with every fiber of my being:

> **We as a Jewish people have come too far, contributed too much to the world, and still have way too much to offer to throw in the towel now.**

Don't get me wrong. I don't think most Jewish organizations believe they're "throwing in the towel." In fact, they'd probably say they're doing great. They think that because people are still showing up, volunteering and donating (maybe not as many, or as much as before, but still...) that all is right with the world.

For some, it's true. They *are* doing great. But for the majority, it's obvious that what they're doing hasn't produced great results. I'd go as far as to say that far too many Jewish organizations live the famous definition of insanity on a regular basis: ***"doing the same thing over and over again,*** *expecting different results,"* and continuing to:

- Repeat unsuccessful patterns.
- Hope that outcomes will improve without any changes in strategy.
- Hire mediocre staff and recycle the same board members.
- Live in denial that dwindling participation is just a passing phase.

Each of those actions alone could easily derail even the best of efforts. But collectively... **OMG!**

And by continuing to do the same old things, it means those organizations *aren't* doing these things:

- o Striving for excellence.
- o Taking calculated risks.
- o Learning from their mistakes.
- o Holding themselves accountable.

And while that isn't exactly *throwing in the towel*, I'd argue that it's the "windup" before the pitch. So, I think it's time to take a time-out, and go back to the dugout to regroup, because Jewish life is changing by the second. Now, more than ever before, those of us who want to successfully engage Jewish communities need to understand and accept these changes and, as a result, change up the way we go about connecting with them.

Hope is not a strategy, and *same old, same old* just won't cut it, especially these days! I know because I spent nearly 18 years as the Director of Jewish Innovation and Engagement at The Manuel D. and Rhoda Mayerson Foundation, turning old ideas on their heads, experimenting with new methods, challenging the system, and taking some pretty big risks.

I feel incredibly fortunate that The Mayerson Foundation believed in me and was willing to invest in my ideas and out-of-the-box thinking, which brought our shared vision of innovation and change to life. **Because a lot of other people I came across in the organized Jewish community resisted new ideas, despite the repeated failures of the old ones.** I was often told that my thinking was too "pie in the sky." I'd hear, "That's just not how *we* do things around here." *(Right… and how's that been working for you?)*

But fortunately, it didn't matter, because my board, and most especially Foundation President, Neal Mayerson, supported my creativity and encouraged the use of a technique referred to as: **"Blue Sky Thinking."**

Blue Sky Thinking is described as putting all practical limitations, such as money, talent, politics, etc., aside. Unlike a room with a ceiling, which puts a constraint on great ideas, the clear and wide-open sky allows for limitless possibilities to soar—right up to the clouds where said "pies," of *Pie in the Sky* fame, sit patiently waiting for someone to claim them.

And that's exactly what we did!

Blue Sky Thinking was an approach we engaged in religiously, and which brought about some amazing innovations that achieved results often surpassing our own lofty expectations. I owe so many of my best ideas and innovations to Blue Sky Thinking, and I was lucky to have had an organization behind me that championed this kind of thinking... so that innovative ideas had the chance to flourish!

And while it's true that not every bold idea turned into a triumph, getting to work in an environment like that allowed me to take risks and learn as much from the things that *didn't* work as from the things that did -- ultimately helping me develop a keen sense of the ingredients that are critical for success.

Now, thousands of people are engaged in Jewish life thanks to that kind of out-of-the-box thinking, and our refusal to let a ceiling stand in our way! Not only did The Mayerson Foundation embrace this approach wholeheartedly, the Board of Directors put their money where their mouths were, creating an Operating Foundation to unleash the power of dreaming, creating, experimenting, failing, and course-correcting—all on our own terms.

This Operating Foundation enabled me to hire a staff and allowed us to develop and run many very successful initiatives on behalf of the Foundation. These initiatives attracted thousands of unaffiliated Jewish families, teens, young professionals, interfaith couples, and Baby Boomers. Our aim was to help connect our constituents with each other and the Jewish community in ways that were comfortable and meaningful to them…

And it worked… really, really well! (Did I mention it worked really well?!)

As I already noted, over the years we reached many thousands of people. But it's not just that these people came to our programs and events… it's that **they came back** — again and again. And in my book, that's the true measure of success! (and since this *is* my book, I stand by that!).

Our work resulted in numerous marriages, lifelong friendships, congregational and organizational affiliation, committee and board memberships, and leadership roles in the community. I built a reputation as a game-changer by pushing the envelope and by putting a new twist on traditional ways of doing things. And I learned a lot along the way…

- I learned that there are people who will feel threatened by innovative ideas and Blue Sky thinking.

- I learned that pretty much **everyone** is resistant to change to some degree or another. It's just part of human nature.

So, even if you achieve the most stellar results, it might take time to break through, because:
> **no matter how successful you are,**
> **no matter how much good you're doing,**
> **no matter how great the impact on Jewish life,**

there are going to be some people who feel threatened by you.

- I learned there are people who subscribe to the Zero-Sum Game Theory which says, the only way you can win is if I lose. So, spoiler alert: even when you start winning - even when your results can't be denied, some may believe that your success shines a light on their less than amazing results, lack of success or even their failures.

- I learned that change scares the $#!+ out of people. It takes them out of their comfort zone. It forces them to have to work harder and smarter, and essentially, it upsets their "apple cart." And although you can demonstrate the clear advantages of your new and improved Turbo-Charged Apple Cart XJS, it doesn't necessarily mean there won't be some Zero-Sum Gamers out there who will try to put more than a few roadblocks in your path.

But...

- I also learned that there are some amazing people out there too. Likeminded people. People who get it... who are smart and confident in themselves and their ability, and willing to open their minds to new ways of doing things.

So, seek out those people. Surround yourself with those

who support you... those who will root for you to win. They're out there. I promise. And if you stick it out long enough, eventually, even the most resistant will start to see the light and choose not to remain in the dark.

So, stay courageous...
... be persistent...
... and more than anything else,
remain focused.

Because it isn't about who came up with the best idea, who was more successful this time around, or whose apple cart got upended. It's about the very reason for doing all of this to begin with -

It's about the end users, the people who make up the Jewish peoplehood.

It needs to always be about them... because "them" is us! Unfortunately, we the Jewish people are struggling a lot right now. You must feel it too. If you didn't, I doubt you'd be reading this. I'm going to go out on a limb and guess that you work for a Jewish organization, or you contribute your time and/or money to one. Bottom line, you're a stakeholder who cares about the welfare of the Jewish people today and into the future.

I would imagine that somewhere along the line you probably had a "kumbaya" experience at Jewish summer camp, were inspired by an amazing rabbi or teacher, had a transformative experience at your first youth group convention, Hillel Shabbat dinner, trip to Israel, or [fill in the blank].

Me too! I get it. I was bitten by that same bug.

But here's the thing. People like us can fall into a trap. It's easy to lose touch. Think about it. When it comes to engaging your target audience, if you just surround yourself with others just like yourself; people who I call:

Bubble People [noun] / bub.ble peo.ple /…

… People who act like you and think like you - you are bound to lose touch with the very people you want to reach… who, by the way, probably aren't like you, or the rest of your Bubble People pals, at all.

Sooner or later, Bubble People become their own worst enemies. They employ Bubble People thinking. They wear rose colored glasses and subsist on a steady diet of denial. They build a protective structure to insulate themselves and their kind from the cold, harsh realities of a changing world. They live in a world I call the:

Bubblesphere [noun] / bub.ble.sphere /

Bubble People make excuses for low attendance or failed programs and blame the end-user for not showing up or knowing what's good. Even though their programs aren't as popular as they once were, their marketing is no longer making an impact, and their current offerings just aren't cutting it, Bubble People keep putting on programs that *they* like, or that *they think* their target audience will like, with no thought to what their target audience *really would* like.

And, because they live in the Bubblesphere, they can't see that hiring people just like them, programming for people just like them, and serving the needs of people just like them, is one of the biggest reasons participation in their organization is declining.

I guess they just don't realize that once there's no more *them*, there won't be anyone else left either.

And that scares me because:
>Even though Bubble People mean well, and
>Even though they have good intentions, and
>Even though they care very much about them/us/we the Jewish People…

…They still don't seem to get it. I bet it's probably because **they don't even realize they're Bubble People.**

What about you? Are you a Bubble Person? Maybe, reading this, you just discovered you are and didn't even know it.

That's okay - because now that you know, isn't it time you burst out of your bubble?

Are you up for the challenge?

Okay, good. But as I already warned you, it won't be easy – because:

Change is hard.

Change is scary.

Change threatens the status quo.

But you can do this, and I'm going to help. You see... I have the unique advantage of having worked **with** the "Organized Jewish community" (OJC) for nearly 20 years, but not **for** it.

With. For. Potato. Patato. Is there a difference?
There is.

You see, because I didn't work FOR an organization within the Organized Jewish Community, I didn't have most of the constraints that my OJC peers did. They had to play it safe in order to please the funders and donors and constituents who made up the lifeblood of their organizations.

So, I get that it was harder for those in the Organized Jewish Community to take the same kind of risks that I was able to take. While my one and only funder (The Mayerson Foundation) insisted on results - *Measurable... Demonstratable... Replicable results* – plain and simple, I didn't have a lot of donors to placate, or internal politics to play. The better the results, the more my risk-taking was appreciated and encouraged.

I get it was tougher for the OJCers to shoot straight out of the gate with a good idea, because they had layer upon layer of staff and committees and boards with which to contend. Fortunately, I didn't.

I had the good fortune of working in a *Blue Sky* environment, where hierarchies and rubber stamps didn't play into the equation. It was an environment that offered me the opportunity to become an explorer. And while that was an incredible gift, I also viewed it as a responsibility. Here's why:

Since the beginning of time, explorers have ventured into the unknown to discover what lies beyond the safe and the comfortable… something, that understandably, most people don't have the desire or ability to do.

Essentially, the explorer's job is to take the risks *for* us, because, even though we can't go on the journey ourselves, we still want to know what's out there. We still want to benefit from what the explorers uncover when they get there. So, if they're lucky enough to discover new things along the way - things that can shine a light on the unknown, improve our understanding and make our lives better, our jobs easier - isn't it their obligation to share those discoveries… to give us the benefit of their experience? I think it is.

That's why I wrote this book.

I was afforded the incredible and rare opportunity to go on a decades-long expedition that allowed me to take the risk **for** those OJCers… and for you. Yes, I had to navigate some tricky terrain. Yes, I often had to take the "road less traveled." But it also afforded me the opportunity to blaze new trails and forge innovative pathways to Jewish engagement.

Yes. I fell down – but I got back up. Now I'm going to share some of my "field notes" with you so hopefully, you won't have to fall down or take such big risks to reap the rewards.

I wrote this book because I want to help you break the vicious cycle that's preventing you and your organization from reaching its highest potential.

How?

By speaking the truth, by repeating the lessons until they're pounded into your head for good, by pointing out buried landmines that you need to avoid and by providing proven solutions that will help you achieve your goals.

I want to convince you to:
    find the focus,
    muster the courage,
    step up to the challenge
    and have the persistence to go the distance...
and make the kind of change that will keep your organization and the Jewish people in business well into the future.

I want to get you, Dear Reader to "get it." To have a breakthrough, an epiphany, a moment when the lightbulb goes off in your head and you see a path to creating a whole new world filled with impactful Jewish engagement! **So...**

...Let there be light!

CHAPTER ONE
Change or Die.

I know. It sounds pretty dire.

But you don't need to worry, because if you're still reading this it means you're inspired by my challenge and are ready to do what it takes to make real change, per my very explicit warning at the beginning of this book.

So, we're all good. Right?

Okay. But in the likely event that you need help in convincing your board, staff, funders and/or other stakeholders to hop aboard the *Change or Die Express*, here's something you can give them to chew on:

Let's start with your local video store -

Oh, wait –

> You don't have a local video store. I don't either. No one does.

They used to be around every corner, but then, POOF,

they all disappeared. I guess that's because they didn't understand the math:

> **Massive innovation and change to the landscape + refusal to acknowledge said change = giant "Going out of Business" banner**

I guess those video stores thought we'd always be loyal. I guess they didn't think they needed a plan for when we'd inevitably ditch our VHS and DVD players for whatever innovation was just around the bend that made video tapes obsolete.

I guess they thought we'd still prefer to:

> Throw on a sweatshirt (the one with the least amount of *schmutz* on it) fight horrible weather conditions/traffic/crowded parking lots to get there within their hours of operation, browse endlessly through aisle after aisle of videos (praying that when we finally settled on one it would be in stock), rewind the tape and return it to the store before incurring a late fee…

…Rather than just simply subscribing to Netflix.

Shocking that they got that wrong! Who'd have thought that:

Spotify would replace the MP3 Player and iPod…

> …which usurped the CD…

…which displaced the record album…

…that was played on the stereo, which eradicated the record player…

…which ate the phonograph…

…that my father bought for two zuzim.

"Chad gadya, chad gadya."

These obsolete products, and every other product in the universe that has been, or ever will be improved upon, are no longer relevant, because things changed. Many of the owners of these businesses didn't/couldn't/wouldn't change along with them. Period.

However, Bubble People, who live in the Jewish Bubble-sphere, don't always see the similarities. After all, some argue that they're completely different situations. They contend that comparing the awesomeness of Judaism and the Jewish people to a video store is outrageous.

Okay, okay! They might have a point. Video stores and Jewish organizations ARE very different indeed. After all…

…One offered something everyone liked, wanted, and needed. And then one day, things changed, and people got what they liked, wanted and needed from somewhere else. So, they stopped coming, and those places started going out of business.

Eventually, so did video stores.

Okay, so here's the deal. People are people. And that goes for Jewish people just as much as everyone else. **Today, loyalty, guilt and a sense of obligation don't go quite as far as they used to with most people.** That goes for Jewish people, too.

Gone are the days when joining a Temple/Synagogue/Shul, giving to the Jewish Federation and taking part in the Purim Carnival is "just what you do."

We all know Dan. He grew up at Congregation Everytown. He has fond memories of going to services with his family and running around with his friends at the Kiddush afterwards. But now, membership is down. The services haven't changed in decades. There are almost no kids for his kids to run around with. It's not surprising that he and his wife decided not to renew their membership.

People today don't have the time or tolerance for products, services, businesses, or organizations that dig their heels in and refuse to change. We live in a world where we can customize every experience. We're used to getting things the way we want them. And if we don't get what we want - (shrug, oh well!) - we'll move on. We will just search for another product, service, business, or organization out there that has figured out how to deliver precisely what we're looking for.

Once again, as we've already covered – but let's reiterate to be sure it has sunk in –

The same thing applies to Jewish organizations.

Just like sharks have to keep swimming to stay alive, *Jewish organizations must continue to innovate or they will die.*

But that's not to say that Jewish people are suddenly going to stop being Jewish. They won't. At least most won't. At least not right way. But, just like everything else, new delivery systems for giving people what they like, want and need are emerging every day. The question is, what will come along to fill in the gaps that bring a sense of tradition, meaning, and community to Jewish people?

What about your organization? Will it be among those delivery systems?

In order to have a fighting chance, it's critical that you first convince yourself that the old ways of doing things have to change. But that's not enough. It's even more critical that you convince everyone else who needs convincing (decision-makers, board members, funders, stakeholders). Because the sooner your organization climbs aboard the *Change or Die Express*, the more likely it is that your organization will keep the passengers you have and possibly even pick up more along the way!

CHAPTER TWO

Know Thy Audience
(The rest is commentary)

Introducing the lost commandment… the rule, if you only remember one rule, is really the only thing at the end of the day! Because knowing your audience will inform and dictate the changes you are going to make. Because, knowing your audience will allow you to target them directly, build trust, and develop a meaningful relationship with them.

Relationships Matter.
Because relationships = Engagement.

And because knowing your audience means you will know what they:

- o Like.
- o Want.
- o Need.

And that's important. Because, **this isn't about you and your organization** and what *__you__ __think__* or *hope* they'll like, want and need...

IT'S ABOUT THEM. The people. Your audience.

Okay. Don't forget that. Ever. Seriously, don't. Because–

IT'S ALWAYS ABOUT THEM!

Print that out and tape it to your mirror, monitor, phone case, or forehead and realize that

**If you don't make it about them –
you will not succeed.**

The good news is, knowing how to know your audience isn't rocket science. You already do it every single day when it comes to your personal interactions without even realizing it. Think about it. You wouldn't...

- Bring up the idea of going on a Caribbean Cruise the same day your spouse lost his or her biggest account.
- Complain to your girlfriend, who wears a size 18, about how tough it is for you to find clothes in a size 4!
- Serve Sausage Pizza Poppers at a Jewish Federation fundraiser. *(That's career suicide!)*

See what I mean? You gather, sort and select bits of data every day about people around you to avoid conflict, enhance outcomes and just get along in the world.

But, think about it —

Do you do that when it comes to engaging people in Jewish life?

That's the million-dollar question! But the prize for answering it correctly isn't a million dollars. Nor is it an all-expense paid trip, a sports car or even a new washer/dryer. It's the survival of your organization. That's what's at stake here. So, think about this: You wouldn't...

- Expect a group of twenty- and thirty-something's to show up to a New Year's Eve party at a retirement center...

    > *But - you still wonder why no one under the age of 60 ever attends the "Wine and Cheese Mixer" that your Temple Brotherhood has been putting on for the last 25 years!*

- You wouldn't expect pre-teen kids to stop playing video games to toss a beanbag into a bucket to score some fake tattoos and cheap necklaces...

    > *But - you can't seem to put your finger on why there aren't as many families showing up to your Purim Carnival as there used to be...*

- You wouldn't think twice if a 55-year-old woman told you she was starting a second career, or if you saw a 70-year-old man playing tennis...

But - you don't get why these days it's only the 80 and older crowd that shows up for a lunch of boiled chicken and klezmer music in the social hall.

It's time to put two and two together!

It's time to stop living in Denial-ville – that highly populated State of Being in the Bubble-sphere.

It's time to stop guessing, assuming and generalizing about what your audience likes, wants and needs.

It's time to hold yourself accountable...

...even if no one is looking!

It's time to stop wondering why and find out **WHAT THEY REALLY WANT** once and for all!

Well, wonder no more...

CHAPTER THREE
The Circle Game

When it comes to "knowing" your audience (understanding what they like, want and need) you first you have to know "who" the audience is that you're trying to know.

That is… your "target" audience.

There's a reason they're called a "target" audience, because they're who you're aiming at - the people you want to attract so you can keep doing what you're doing and continue to improve upon it. Remember those swimming sharks!

There are several circles on a target. The middle one is the bullseye, or in this case, your **Primary Target Market**. The others are the concentric circles that surround the bullseye. They make up the **Secondary Target Markets**. The bullseye and concentric circles are segments of your market that can/will/should change places depending upon the situation.

If you were holding a **fundraising dinner** for your organization's new *Max and Miriam Schmagegi Career Services Division*, your Primary Target Market wouldn't be Jewish young adults. Instead, it would be community and business leaders, current contributors, wealthy funders and of course, friends and family of the Schmagegi's. People in a position to give money… *Right?* Remember after all, it's a fundraiser. So, right!

However, if you were throwing a **networking event** to introduce *the Max and Miriam Schmagegi Career Services Division* to a new audience who you hope will *use* this service, your bullseye *would* likely be Jewish young adults.

With any given program you have to know who's in the bullseye. If you don't know, you need to, because…

…different target markets require different marketing strategies,

because…

… different target audiences like, want, and need different things!

For example, you might segment your markets by:

- o Age
- o Gender
- o Geography
- o Level of Jewish literacy
- o Level of Jewish connection/identification/interest
- o Or anything else that makes sense.

But remember this:

**You can't hit every circle on the target
with just one arrow.**

Case in Point #1

A few years ago, the Program Director of a large Jewish organization showed me an oversized postcard mailer he had just sent out to his membership database of over 2,500.

"Mix and Mingle without the Jingle"

December 24th at 6:30pm

JCC Multipurpose Room

For ages 21 and older.

Delicious food, musical entertainment

and specialty drinks.

Free with an RSVP.

Program Director ("PD"): "What do you think?" (beaming).

Me: "The title is really clever!" (You can always find something positive to say!).

PD: "Thanks! (beaming even more). Do you think a lot of

people will come?"

Me: "Honestly..." (I am always honest to a fault about stuff like this which sometimes gets me into hot water).

PD: "Of course!"

Me: *(OY! Here goes nothin')* "… Based on experience, I worry that you're going to be disappointed in the turnout." *(See what I mean about the honesty thing?).*

PD: "Seriously? (beaming turns to bemusement). "I mean, c'mon, Jewish people have nothing else to do on Christmas Eve. It can't fail! No offense, but I think it's going to be huge!"

Me: "None taken. I hope you're right." (OMG! This thing is going to sink faster than the Titanic!).

Turns out I was wrong. It actually sank faster than the Egyptian army in the Red Sea! Turns out they ended up cancelling the event due to a mere seven RSVP's.

I hate when things like this happen. Because they don't have to. It's a shame that all the time, energy and money put into this effort was wasted. So, how did I know? How was I so sure it wasn't going to succeed? Simple.

The Program Director didn't identify a target audience.

But - you might argue - the invitation clearly said it was for ages 21 and over. And I would counter that you need to read more carefully because you might have forgotten what we just covered. Remember?... It's not possible to hit every circle on the target with just one arrow.

I would also point out that if you don't identify the bull-seye, you are going to break your back picking up all the arrows you just shot straight into the wind. So, let's break it down. Here's why I was able to predict what was going to happen: *I knew that —*

The twenty- and thirty-somethings wouldn't come because they'd think that it was going to be a party for a bunch of old people their parents' and/or grandparents' ages. After all, it just said it was for people 21 and up. That could mean ANYTHING! And really, are you even kidding me? 6:30pm? That's when most twenty- and thirty-somethings are just getting started for the day.

The forty-somethings wouldn't come because if they were going to get a sitter and go out for the night, they'd want to hit a cool club, or just go to a movie. Plus, they wouldn't be sure if it was a party for young singles or the geriatric crowd.

The Baby Boomers wouldn't come because they'd think it's going to be a party for a bunch of "kids" their kids' age.

The 75+ crowd wouldn't come because, are you even kidding me? 6:30pm? That's when this age group is getting ready to turn in for the night!

Plus, there's the matter of deadly ambiguity:

"Delicious food" – Is that dinner, heavy appetizers, dessert? What kind of food is it?

"Musical entertainment" – Is that a Klezmer band, a Jazz Quartet, or a DJ?

"Specialty drinks" – Are we talking root beer floats, rum and Coke, or Judah Maccabee Martinis? Does that mean liquor, just beer and wine, punch… what?

And then there's this:

Just because it's Christmas Eve doesn't mean every Jewish person is sitting around with nothing to do. Not only do many Jews volunteer to help in the Gentile community in any number of ways, it's no secret that many are also in relationships with, or are married to, someone of another faith, or to someone who didn't grow up Jewish. Hence there may be extended family obligations among other things. We need to acknowledge that when planning programs and events during holidays such as Christmas and Easter and adjust our expectations per the makeup of our intended audience, **#wakeuptothereality.**

Reminder: When you try to reach everyone, you won't reach anyone!

Reminder: Different target audiences like, want, and need different things (there's that old ditty again!)

If you don't identify your target audience you won't be able to pinpoint what they like, want, and need, which will force your programming to be generic or vague in an attempt to please everyone. But... **THAT DOESN'T WORK!** Because... *you can't hit every circle on the target with just one arrow*. (There's that other old ditty again!)

Okay, you get it.

So, go figure out who your audience is because it's time to find out what they like, want and need.

CHAPTER FOUR
Hitting the Bullseye

In the last chapter we talked targets. Now, let's talk **arrows**.

Remember, the *target* represents your audiences -- the bullseye is the market segment you hope to hit. And in order to do that, you need a streamlined and precision-crafted *arrow*.

So, for example, if Millennials are the bullseye, you need your arrow to home in with great care on the event or program that you're planning. It's critical you don't miss. But how are you going to go about doing it? Actually, it's surprisingly simple...

Ask them.

That's right. Just ask them!

Well... the word "just" might be oversimplifying it a bit.

I've created a whole unscientific science around the "asking" and around the way it should be done if you want to obtain the best, most useful data without having to spend tons of time and money. So, while it's a simple concept, it does require more than just going up to people and asking them. And while in some cases, that's a legit way of doing it, there are better, more effective methods.

So, stick with me because I'm going to lay it all out. But first...

A word from our sponsor:

Hey you! That's right. YOU. The one with the spring in your step. The one who's heading down the road toward innovative change and high impact engagement? Great job! You're making progress -

But if you don't pay attention to the pitfalls all around you, you could go off course and that would be really tragic because you're getting so close.

Introducing, **Trap Tracker**: the perfect tool to help you navigate your way through unfamiliar terrain. **Trap Tracker** is an early warning system that alerts you to all the traps that threaten to throw you back into the Bubble-sphere. When it detects that you're about to step into something you shouldn't, it emits a high-pitched sound guaranteed to burst any Bubbles out there that attempt to beckon you back inside.

But, don't take our word for it, listen to what these satisfied customers have to say:

Marsha Goldman:

"Hi! I was just like you. I was hot on the trail to finding out what my target audience was looking for when suddenly I thought… wait, **"I don't have to ask them because I *am* them."** After all, I'm a 38-year-old Jewish woman with two kids who runs the Youth and Family department at my JCC. Don't I already know what every other thirty-something Jewish woman with kids wants? But then my *Trap Tracker* went off and I realized I was being a Bubble Person and I woke up to reality. *Thanks Trap Tracker for getting me back on track!"*

Seth Joseph:

I sit on the board of my local Hillel. At our meetings, when the Program Director updates us on the number of students who attend monthly events, everyone in the room oohs and ahhs, and then we move on to new business, basking in the glow of how great we're doing! At the last meeting everyone was marveling that 63 people came to the Welcome Barbeque for First Year Students. I thought, WOW, our Hillel is off to a great start for the year! But then my *Trap Tracker* went off, causing me to actually ask, **"How many of those who attended were 'Jewish first year' students?"**

Come to find out that four were staff members, three were student interns and forty-two were upperclassmen and grad students who were already highly engaged in Hillel. Only fourteen were first year students, and of those, **just nine were Jewish**. On a campus with approximately 1,700 Jewish first years, that number represented just a tiny fraction of our potential target population! But thanks to *Trap Tracker*, I started a trend. Now board members aren't just taking every report at face value. Knowing that questions like that are going to come up, the staff has been more intentional about analyzing the data and making changes to their programs based on the results! *Thanks Trap Tracker for getting us back on track!*

Don't fall into another tricky trap. Get Trap Tracker today and get back on track!

Okay, back to our regularly scheduled program…

So, now you get it. When it comes to finding out what your target audience likes, wants and needs, guessing, assuming and/or projecting your own views or agenda is not the right approach. So, what should you do?

Glad you asked! – Actually, it's such an important question that I'm going to devote the rest of the book to answering it.

So, PAY ATTENTION…

Pam's Three Essential Rules

for creating highly successful, high impact programming,
"By the People, For the People"

1. **Ask them what they want.**
2. **Hear what they have to say.**
3. **Give them what they ask for.**

I get it. These three things seem almost silly in their simplicity. But seriously, it took me nearly a decade to boil everything I had learned down to three bite-sized nuggets that are easy to swallow and work every single time (disclaimer: only if you follow the instructions).

So, grab your bow and arrow. It's time to head out to the archery range…

CHAPTER FIVE
Ask Them What They Want

Data Talks.

Data can have a lot to say and it will tell you things if you listen. But when it talks, you have to be ready to walk the walk.

Once you collect it, you'll need to analyze it. Once you've analyzed it, you'll need to act on it. And acting on it is going to bring about change. Do you remember what I said about change?

Change is hard.
Change is scary.
Change threatens the status quo.

So, gear yourself up and let's go get us some data!

There are several ways you can "ask people what they want":

The one-on-one conversation method –

In person or on the phone, having the chance to have an in-depth discussion with individuals in your target audience is never a bad thing. If you have the time and bandwidth to take this on, you should. However, in true *Trap Tracker* tradition, you need to be sure of two things: you're engaging the right folks, and, that you're able to speak to enough of them to matter. Otherwise, you'll just be wasting your time and theirs!

Reminder:

Don't be a Bubble Person.

So how does this tactic rate? If you have the resources, this is a great **complement** to one or both of the methods below. For that reason, I give it a B-.

The questionnaire/survey method – This is a great way

to collect data from, a.) people who love your organization and, b.) people who don't. There are usually very few in-betweeners who will care even a little. So typically, it's the folks on either end of the spectrum who will bother to complete it.

In many ways, we are not all that different from one another. We rarely complete surveys that come into our inboxes, unless of course, we… a.) love the company/product/organization/candidate or, b.) hate them. But most of the time, neither of the above. We just don't bother. Right?

So, even though it's valuable to get ideas and input from

both sides of the spectrum, you need a lot more than lovers and haters if you're going to hang your hat on this data.

Lastly, surveys don't allow you to follow a trail down a different path or change your line of questioning if something amazing starts to emerge that you didn't expect. And, oh yeah... one last "lastly" (sorry!). Sometimes, organizations publish community studies and other survey data which, whether by accident or on purpose, creates a false sense of success and security in the Bubblesphere.

For example, *survey says...* 48% of people in the Everytown Jewish community are affiliated with a congregation, which is 10% higher than other like-sized communities around the country.

When they read that, everyone in Everytown probably thinks:

Congregations in Everytown are doing great because affiliation is high. Compared to what, we don't know. However, we do know that it's 10% higher than Othertowns' affiliation rates, so that's good enough for us. All the rabbis, boards and committees at the temples and synagogues in town can rest on their laurels and stay exactly the same. Good job guys! Everytown rules!

Oh, but wait! Don't get ready to dance the Hora just yet...

...Here's what they didn't report: Of those who are affiliated, 85% have only attended a service or program **two times or less** in the last 12 months, and that included the High Holidays, Bar/Bat Mitzvahs, funerals and weddings.

Wonder why they forget to mention that?

Because if they had mentioned that, I bet the big takeaway might have looked more like this:

On average 85% of all people in the Everytown Jewish community who belong to a congregation only attend lifecycle events or an annual High Holiday service and aren't engaged or interested in whatever else their congregation offers. Maybe these congregations should change the way they're doing things.

Oops! There's the "C" word again. Change. It just keeps popping up all over the place! I mean, you get it's hard, scary, threatening and yada, yada, yada. Could that be why some organizations end up sticking their heads in the sand even after investing hundreds of thousands of dollars (yes, that's how much they really cost!) in studies like this?

Ultimately, the organization that commissioned the survey needs to take responsibility for reporting it fully and responsibly and be ready to act based on the results... even if they're not pretty. And remember this. If you're going to gather data, it needs to be for the right reasons.

I've seen more than a few organizations that cherry picked the responses so they could paint a particular picture for funders, their constituents, or community at large. This allowed them to "shoot the arrows against the wall and then draw the target." Pretty clever... but guess what? Reality came back to bite them in the you know what.

Because data doesn't lie.

Over the next few years, the congregations in that community started to lose more and more members because the people who belonged out of guilt or obligation were dying off, and their programs and services and other offerings weren't resonating with many younger people who didn't share the "guilt and obligation" gene. So, how did just reporting on half of the story help anyone in the end? It didn't, because...

> **...Pulling the wool over your eyes to fool yourself or creating smoke and mirrors to try and fool others, is just plain foolish.**

Don't get me wrong. Crafted and reported correctly, community studies, questionnaires and surveys can be valuable tools in helping funders and policy makers understand demographics, geography, social service needs, and more, but they're often very expensive, difficult to word and properly weight, and are limited in their ability to zero in on people's attitudes, interests, likes and wants (and that's what we're after here!).

So how does this approach rate? I give it a C-. It just sets off my **Trap Tracker** a little too much. If you don't have the time, money and resources needed to go with more than one methodology, I'm just saying, think long and hard before going down the questionnaire/survey road for this purpose.

So, what's the methodology that I believe will give you the biggest bang for your "know thy audience" buck? The one that rates an A+ in my book? Allow me to introduce you to the most overlooked, underappreciated treasure in the trove...

CHAPTER SIX

Focus Pocus...

The Magical Potion for Success

Poor, poor underrated Focus Group. No one notices you, but you have so much potential. You're easy going, super reliable and always full of surprises! Sure, you have your serious side, but you can also be a lot of fun. You don't want much. You just want people to be open and honest, and in return, you will give them everything they could ask for – and more. I won't let them keep you in a corner any longer. Your time to shine has come!

It's no secret that focus groups are my number one, sure-fire, go-to tactic for taking a gut check, getting new ideas, refreshing old ones, engaging the target audience and so much more. Once you see what focus groups can do for you, you won't be able to help but make them your partner in developing primo programs and perfectly targeted marketing. Done correctly, focus groups result in high-impact audience attraction, retention and engagement! To help understand why I'm such a believer in them, consider the following:

Case in Point #2

(Names have been changed to protect the Bubble People)

A few years ago, I did some consulting work with a synagogue I'll call Congregation Everytown. Over the past decade the congregation lost about a third of its members and the religious school had dwindled to a handful of students. The average age of said members was 65 years old. They weren't getting any new members and were in grave danger of going out of business. I asked their leadership what they thought was the cause of the challenges they were having.

"We put on all these programs, but the younger members don't come. (Please note, by "younger" they were referring to people in their 50's and 60's.) For example, our Sisterhood had its Bagel and Book Club Breakfast last Tuesday. Joyce served her famous whitefish salad! Sure, we talk about the book, but it's more of an excuse to get together and schmooze a little. We've been doing this for 25 years but it's probably not going to continue for much longer because the younger girls can't be bothered. We were busy with things when we were their age too, but somehow, we managed to make time for what mattered. They obviously have better things to do. Humph!"

Here's another…

"The young people probably think they don't HAVE TO join a synagogue anymore. They can go on the internet and find a rabbi who will do anything they need, a wedding, bris, baby naming, funeral… It's all about them. (Please note, in case you missed the nuance, their sarcastic, "it's all about them" is the direct opposite of my, "it's all about them," in Chapter Two.) They don't want to pay dues or get involved. So, when there are no more synagogues in town, they'll be sorry! "

And so on, and so on, and so on. They couldn't see the irony. But you can see it. ***Right?***

You can see that if their congregation goes down in flames it won't be because the young people didn't want to get involved. And you get that the only ones who are going to be **sorry** are the Congregation Everytown congregants themselves because they've made it all about "themselves." You see, if they had actually made it about the people they didn't have, (the ones they might have been able to attract if they had ever bothered to ask them what they wanted) Congregation Everytown probably wouldn't be experiencing this sharp decline.

But every time I asked the congregants if they had ever asked the people who never came to anything what they wanted, the answer was either, *"If they don't come how can we ask them?"* or *"Why would we do that?"* Or the best one of all; *"It's a waste. They don't know what's good."*

But the real kicker was when I said I'd like to conduct a focus group to find out how to improve the congregation's ability to attract new people…

"You don't need to. We already did that about a year ago. Half the congregation showed up. We broke into groups, and Maury, a congregant and former corporate big shot (he was an accountant at a big company which somehow qualified him to take the lead, but okay!) *facilitated the whole thing. He asked everyone what they wanted, and he wrote all the ideas on a big easel.*

We got great stuff. We now have a "Study with the Rabbi" session every month after Shabbat services. Ask Abe about that. He's one of the seven regulars who swears by it! Miriam had the idea of having an off-site event, so we had a Picnic in the Park over the summer which was fun. We also decided the annual Holiday Gift Bazaar was just too much work, so we formed a committee to investigate some alternative fundraising ideas. Maury probably kept the easel sheets, so he can give those to you to look at."

Okay…Even though the focus group they thought they were having was really more like a Bubblesphere Brainstorm Session, in the end, it was great that:

- A lot of congregants showed up.
- They came up with a lot of ideas, some of which they had already put into action.

That was a good thing. Right?

Absolutely, if the goal of said focus group/brainstorm session was to come up with ways to keep the core group happy, attract more people just like them to do things people just like them wanted to do. All legitimate goals no doubt.

But that *wasn't* the goal.

The goal was to come up with ways to STAY ALIVE, which of course meant keeping the people they already had (especially those who rarely if ever came to anything), but as importantly, or even more so, coming up with ways to attract people who **WEREN'T** just like them - people who wanted something different. **Because just doing more of what they were already doing wasn't bringing those new people in.**

I felt like I was watching the Bubblesphere's newest TV game show, where only hardcore members of Congregation Everytown get to compete for who can come up with more ways to keep potential new members from joining:

> **It's easy and it's fun! Watch as Shirley throws out the first zinger:** *"They don't even know what they want."* **But then Myron comes in with a decisive**, *"If they don't show up to give their ideas then they can't complain when we do things our way"* **to take the lead. But wait, Fred buzzes in at the last second for the steal...** *"Would it kill them to come to synagogue once in a while?"*

The game gets more challenging by the second as more and more members drop out, leaving just the die-hard contestants to go head to head for bragging rights and the chance to say they were the one who got to turn off the lights!

I joke… but there are serious consequences when you play this game. There are no winners- only losers, because…

…If you only ask the people you have, you'll never get the people you don't have. Period.

Like I said, they couldn't see it. I don't blame them. It just didn't occur to the "Old Guard" that their stranglehold on the reins was driving the mass exodus of the younger members. They didn't see that their "our way or the high-way" sensibility was responsible for their problems.

These people were passionate about the congregation they had built up over the decades. This place was responsible for giving them their fondest memories and lifelong friendships. It's where they attended lifecycle events and celebrations and where they found comfort in times of sadness. It was their sanctuary from the chaos of the outside world. These were the people who schlepped and set-up and supported the building fund. They raised money for camp and day school scholarships and populated the services, classes, social events and fundraisers.

I totally got it. But unfortunately, if I couldn't help them "get it," and soon, it would be time to shut off the lights for good. It was time to call on my trusted and loyal companion, the Focus Group, as a first step in helping them get on the road to recovery!

Stay tuned… I'm going to circle back around and tell you what happened with Congregation Everytown. Before I do that though, I want to introduce you to a little formula I came up with that I think you'll find helpful when conducting your own focus groups.

The 3M Company invented a game changing formula that made creating reminders as simple as pressing a little square of paper onto any surface. Brilliant! My formula isn't going to send me into early retirement, but it has been a great tool in helping me remember the recipe for bringing out the best, and getting the most, out of any focus group. It has been a game changer for me and so many others, and it can be for you too:

Pam's 4M Formula for Foolproof Focus Groups:

- o **Mix**
- o **Marketing**
- o **Money**
- o **Method**

Okay, let's break down the components…

CHAPTER SEVEN
M is for Mix

As we saw in the previous case study, getting the right mix of people is a critical component of a successful focus group. If done incorrectly, it can lead to results that couldn't be more misleading. **So, if you don't have the right mix of people – don't bother!**

I realize I'm beating you over the head. But knowing your audience is so important and getting the right representative mix of people to "speak for" that audience is paramount – as exemplified in this cautionary tale...

Case in Point #3

(Fictious yet representative of so many real cases I have seen)

Once upon a time...

...in a land not so far away, there was a company called Gotwind Games that had been manufacturing high-end Mahjong sets for nearly 100 years.

When Gil Gotwind, great grandson of the founder, took over the reins, he was distressed to learn that over the past decade sales had dipped dramatically. A market analysis revealed that the majority of Maj enthusiasts were women in their late 70's and 80's.

Younger people were just not taking to this game like they used to. The study cited busy lifestyles, that more women were working outside the home than ever before, and in general, that the game no longer had the same appeal as it used to have. People seemed to be more interested in spending the little free time they had working out, meeting up for lattes, getting involved in the latest social action project and engaging in more fast-paced activities.

What was Gil Gotwind to do?

He couldn't fathom the idea of closing the business that had been so good to his family for generations. But he knew he had to do something soon or he wouldn't have a choice. Lucky for Gil, his brilliant young assistant, Gail, turned out to be great at inventing games. One day, she came up with something innovative and cool that combined traditional fun with a high-tech twist. She thought it might open the door to a whole new customer base.

"You're a genius, Gail. I think this is just what we need to save the business," exclaimed Gil. "Let's test it out first to see if it will fly?" Gil wisely said. After all, he didn't want to jump from the frying pan into the fire. Smart!

So, the very next day, Gil sent a letter out to everyone in town who had purchased one of his Gotwind Maj sets over the past 5 years. He invited them to come give their feedback on this clever new product he hoped to manufacture very soon.

Thirty people showed up -- and they gave Gil their opinion alright. Sadly, it turned out they just didn't get it. The tiles were different, the designs were weird and the app that they had to sync to their phones in order to play the game was way too complicated.

"Forget it," they cried. "This game will never catch on."

So, Gil dropped the idea. After all, his customers had spoken. It seemed like it had so much potential. Good thing he hadn't rushed into production! PHEW! Crisis averted.

Unfortunately, just a year later, Gil had to have a going out of business sale. He took the portrait of Great Grandpa Gotwind off the wall and said goodbye to 100 years of hard work and family history.

The story doesn't have a happy ending for Gil. Poor, poor Gil. Too bad the only people from whom he solicited feedback were his current customers; tech-adverse octogenarians who clearly liked things just the way they were! If you're thinking that this sounds like the case I just cited regarding a certain Congregation Everytown, you're definitely catching on!

But the story has a happier ending for Gail. She decided to do it her way. She hand-picked several groups of twenty-somethings to come to a few Game Night Focus groups where she test-marketed her new game idea and got lots of other great ideas from the participants for how to make it even better.

Turns out, it tested through the roof. Gail listened carefully to their suggestions for ways to improve upon the original idea. She received their feedback for how much they'd be willing to pay, their input for how she should market it to their friends and others like them. She did what they suggested and then took it to the bank, literally. Now Gail is the proud CEO of Millennial Games. And get this, her, **Tech, Tac, Tile** is the hottest game sensation since Maj -- and is played by young people everywhere.

Go Gail!

So, what happened here? How did things go so wrong for Gil, but so right for Gail? Clearly Gail had a great product. So, what gives?

What gives is that Gil made a grave mistake. Gil sent a letter out to his *current* customers, with an open call to participate in a focus group... just like Congregation Everytown did.

And who were Gil's current customers? They were the people who had purchased a Maj set over the past five years who, the market analysis revealed, were people in their 70's and 80's. Wait, that's basically who Congregation Everytown's current customers were too.

But even though Gil was hoping to find a new product to appeal to a much younger audience in order to save his business, **he listened to the opinions of people who couldn't begin to relate to said audience.** Bottom line… they didn't get it… they didn't want it… they weren't having it. Hmmm, sounds like a certain congregation I know. (Paging Congregation Everytown… your mirror is calling, and it wants you to hold it up to yourself!).

If only Gil understood that allowing his current customers to dictate what was best, was NOT in his company's best interest. Allowing his current customers to decide that just because something wasn't in *their* comfort zone, didn't fit with *their* interests and wasn't in *their* wheelhouse, would be his ultimate undoing. If only!

But Gail got it. Gail knew that she had to do a little work in order to get the right group of people to the table. But when she did…

…when she heard what they had to say and did what they suggested, she succeeded.

What's the moral of the story?

Gil Gotwind didn't deserve what he got. But in the end, he got what he got because he didn't get it. It's better to be like Gail, who got feedback from the group she wanted to get, and hence, Gail became a "game" changer... *(get it?)* ☺

The End.

So, what have we learned so far?

Don't put out an *open call* to your current constituency, unless you're just trying to come up with ways of keeping them happy, which is a legitimate thing to do. But, if you're trying to get new people who you don't have, don't count on your current "super fans," who've already drunk the Kool-Aid, to give you what you need.

It won't help you to go down that road. Because, the idea is to **Know Thy Audience.** Knowing your audience can best be achieved by asking people who are of the group you are **trying to attract.** But, due to the fact that you're *trying to attract* them, it means that

YOU DON'T HAVE THEM... YET.

So, in this case, you need to invite the people to your focus group who (wait for it) ... *you don't have yet!*

But you already know that. You already know that if you just ask the people you've got, you'll never get the ones you don't. (That old thing again?) So, it stands to reason that when you go to construct your focus group, you have to include the right participants.

That means you have to be picky.

That means you have to hand pick your participants so you're sure to have representation, **not from the audience you already have, but from the target audience you are trying to get.** Here's how I constructed the mix of people and focus groups for Congregation Everytown to find out what they should be doing to attract and retain younger members:

- **Group #1** – People between the ages of 45-60 who belonged to the congregation but *rarely, if ever,* came to anything. It was easy to identify these folks. I sat down with a membership list and a few Congregation Everytown Super Fans who came to everything, so they could tell me who from the list fit the bill.

- **Group #2** – People between the ages of 40-55 who were members of the synagogue but had dropped out. This was easy too. I just pulled from Congregation Everytown's mile-long list of lapsed members.

- **Group #3** - People between the ages of 35-49 who lived within a 10-mile radius and had never belonged to Congregation Everytown and were not currently members of any synagogue. More difficult, but almost everyone knows people in this category, so it was a matter of asking around.

I Dare Ya!

I was able to recruit between 8-12 people per group, which is the optimal range for a focus group. However, in order to end up with that number of people I had to invite 15-20 people per group to get 8-12 viable participants. In almost every case, ***getting the names is the easy part, getting them there is a whole different ballgame.*** This was no exception! Don't forget... these aren't core members of the congregation who care deeply about what goes on there. In fact, I'd contend it's quite the opposite. So how did I get them there? Stay tuned...

CHAPTER EIGHT
M is for Marketing

People are busy.
They pick.
They choose.
They prioritize.

If you want to increase the chance that you'll end up getting the people you **need** in order to even make conducting a focus group worthwhile, you have to find ways of enticing those people to participate. That's where marketing comes into play.

Marketing is the business of promoting and selling a product or service. And while I could (and probably will!) write an entire book on how to effectively market the programs/events/services that will ultimately result from your focus group(s), you first need to get the people you don't have to show up to said focus group.

When it comes to putting on a fundraiser, most organizations know that in order to successfully market it to potential guests (that is, sell seats and tables) they'll need to find a great venue that will attract the biggest donors. They'll need a draw, such as an amazing speaker or entertainer, and they'll have to carefully consider what kind of food and beverages will help seal the deal. The same goes for a focus group. Seriously. It's basically the same, just on a smaller scale.

Because, people are busy. They pick. They choose. They prioritize. So you must be able to offer something "marketable" or chirping crickets are going to be the only focus group participants you will be able to attract.

Think about it…

…**Holding the event in a windowless boardroom in a building that your potential focus groupers aren't interested in stepping foot into isn't exactly going to inspire participation.** Location is important for lots of reasons, as we will explore further in just a few pages. But where you host it will be one of several critical factors in your ability to effectively market it to your target audience.

…Think about it. You work all day. You often have evening meetings during the week for your job or for a volunteer board or committee. Your weekends are filled with family obligations and errands, fundraising dinners and so much more. Who has time to breathe, let alone go to a focus group in an uninviting setting?

One day, you get an invitation to participate in a focus group for the **National Bad Disease Organization** (NBDO)

Subject line: We need your help

Dear Ari,

I would like to invite you to take part in a focus group on Thursday, May 5th at 6pm in Conference Room B at our offices. The focus group should last no longer than one and a half hours. Refreshments will be provided. The focus group will give you an opportunity to learn about our organization and give us your views on some new programs we are hoping to unveil in the next few months. If you would like to take part, please let us know by contacting Josephine Magilicutty...

You think NBDO is probably a worthwhile organization. However, you've never contributed to their cause. You've never participated in one of their Walks or given them much thought. So, spending the little free time you have to sit in some conference room, over a bowl of pretzels and a can of Diet Coke, to help out an organization you know you should care about, but you really don't, doesn't even rate on your list of priorities – not now. Not ever. So...

...Delete.

Here's the dilemma. You know you need to talk to people who don't necessarily want to talk to you. But if you can't get them to talk to you then you're right back where you started. ARGH! Now what?

Okay, so we've established it's going to be a challenge. But you're up to the task. You can do this. Do you know why? Because you know that…

YOU HAVE TO KNOW YOUR AUDIENCE.

And that

IT'S ALWAYS ABOUT THEM.

And furthermore,

PEOPLE ARE BUSY. THEY PICK. THEY CHOOSE. THEY PRIORITIZE.

So, you will figure out how to make it worth their while. You will figure out how to market the focus group to them. You will show them what's in it for them: your picky, choosy, target audience. You already know what to do. You know because I just told you.

Just "ASK".

That's right. *Ask a few people who are representative of the folks you want to come to your focus group.* Did you get that?

If you want people who are weakly engaged and/or disenfranchised or unaffiliated with your organization to come to your focus group, then find a few of them and just ask what would motivate them, and others like them to become *actual* focus groupers.

Don't guess.
Don't ever guess.
And never assume.
Just ask!

As the Director of Jewish Innovation and Engagement for nearly two decades, I could have rested on my laurels. It was tempting to rely on my instincts for what would work. But I never allowed myself or my staff to bank on educated guesses or project our own ideas when it came to attracting our target audience, even when it came to getting a representative sample of them to come to a focus group to talk about how to attract our target audience!

This is the response I got from a few twenty- and thirty-somethings when I asked what it would take to get them to come to a focus group to help an organization they didn't care much, or at all, about. Here's what they said:

- Money! (No joke. Paying me would work!).
- Good food.
- Alcohol.
- It can't be a sales pitch.
- It can't feel judgmental.
- I have to be able to say what I really think and not worry about offending anyone.

So, after getting a good sense for what might work, straight from a few of the horses' mouths, I put together an email invitation:

<u>Subject Line:</u> Dinner & Drinks at [*insert name of trendy restaurant here*] on us!

Dear Ari,

We want to know what you REALLY think! As someone who is not affiliated with a Temple or Synagogue your feedback, input and ideas are extremely valuable to our Congregation as we work to improve our appeal to people just like you.

We **<u>are not</u>** asking you to become a member or attend our services or programs. Instead, **we are inviting you, along with a select group of your peers, to join us for a brief, one-time event:**

Dinner & a drink on us in a private room at
[*Insert name of trendy restaurant here*]
Sunday, May 5th at 6pm.

We are eager to hear your honest opinions (really!) and promise a fun evening in ***a judgment- and expectation-free zone!*** No strings attached. We promise! And we also promise to have you out of there by 8:30pm!

As a participant, you will receive a $25 Visa Gift card as a token of our appreciation for your important contribution to this effort. **Please <u>RSVP</u> by May 1st to reserve your spot**. If you have any questions, don't hesitate to reply to this email, or contact me directly at 555-123-4567. Thank you for your consideration. I look forward to hearing from you soon.

Hope to see you on the 5th! Pam Saeks, Chief Strategy Consultant

Now let's revisit our list from above. Does this letter check all the boxes?:

- **Money** – Check. Visa gift cards all around!
- **Good food** – Check. It's being held at a restaurant that a lot of people like, and we're serving…
- **…Alcohol** – Check. We were clear in saying Dinner and a Drink
- **It can't be a sales pitch** – Check. No language telling them how they can learn about the congregation or that anyone expects them to join or do anything more than give their feedback.
- It can't feel judgmental – Check. - It says, point blank: it's a *judgment- and expectation-free zone!*
- I have to be able to say what I really think and not worry about offending anyone – Check. – Language like, *We want to know what you really think* and *We are eager to hear your honest opinions (really!)* does the trick. (Warning: If you say it, you have to mean it!).
- And, finally, even though they didn't mention this in so many words, it's still human nature to want to feel special! Adding this line: ***"We are inviting you***

and a select group of your peers..." definitely checks that box.

Yes. This worked. However, don't think for a minute that I didn't have to circle back around with at least half of them, make some personal calls, ask people who knew people to make calls, and even send out a second set of emails to a new group of potential participants (friends and acquaintances of the folks who did RSVP) to get the right number and mix of people to say yes.

No matter how many bells and whistles you offer, getting the right mix of people, especially those who aren't interested in what you're selling, isn't easy. So... the way you market your focus group really matters!! Because in the end, be it as *seemingly* insignificant as attracting people to populate a focus group or enticing donors to attend a five-hundred-person fundraiser, you need great marketing. And great marketing starts with what? It starts with...

...Knowing your audience.

So, what happened with Congregation Everytown?

The conclusion to Case in Point #3

The focus groups we conducted resulted in a wealth of great ideas, as well as some constructive criticism for what could be done to make it easier and more appealing for any and all to participate in Congregation Everytown offerings.

They were honest about the things they didn't like and willing to help bring some of their own ideas to life. Congregation Everytown was pleasantly surprised that so much of what came out of the focus groups was reasonable and doable. They weren't able to do everything that was suggested right away, but because they were finally willing to "hear" what was being said they were able to make a lot of the necessary changes, and as a result, great things started happening, such as:

The High Holiday Family Farmer's Market, complete with local vendors, a petting zoo and other activities for all ages brought Congregation Everytown's grounds and parking lot to life, attracting nearly 1,000 people in an afternoon and resulting in greater awareness and interest in Congregation Everytown. It's now an annual event!

The Shabbat JAMboree, brought music lovers together, along with their instruments, for a lively Saturday service that filled the synagogue with a rich mixture of sounds and a renewed sense of spirited and spiritual fun. (It's now a regular monthly service which attracts hundreds of people from across the community and neighboring cities.)

The Pancake and PJ Party Shabbat Dinner for families attracted 84 participants, mostly comprised of non-members. (Many of the participants are now members!). The dinner featured breakfast for dinner, a family Shabbat service with flashlights and puppets, songs, stories and other activities. Now, family Shabbat dinners with kid-friendly themes are a regular part of the program at Congregation Everytown, which has picked up a big following among young families in the community!

In the end, 17 of the original 27 focus group participants who were not already members of Congregation Everytown became members that year. By their very presence, they were able to bring a younger more contemporary sensibility to the congregation. As a result, the congregation reversed the membership decline they had been experiencing.

Their numbers are steadily growing and some of the younger members started joining committees, taking on leadership roles and are making the kind of change that has started attracting more people like them.

What about the older members, the ones who were resistant to change? You might be surprised to know that they can't stop boasting about how many young people and families have recently joined. More of them come to services on a regular basis because they actually love seeing all the kids who have brought so much happiness and life back to the congregation. All of this was a result of opening themselves up to new ideas and even some criticism. It was about getting out of the Blame Game and looking in the mirror and taking responsibility for their own destiny. It took some doing, but Congregation Everytown got it…

…What about you? Do you get it too? Are you still up for

the challenge? Because it's not going to be easy, which is why most organizations don't engage in the "asking" or at best, they just get feedback from who they've got and hope for the best.

But you and I know that hope is not a strategy, and if you only ask the people you have you won't get the people you don't. *(Hello old friend!)* I hope you're not thinking, ***Oy! this is too hard.*** But if you are, it's better that you know now.

So, what'll it be? Because if you're starting to have second thoughts about going down this road, it's going to get bumpier right about *now!*

CHAPTER NINE
M is for Money

This "M" permeates through all of those "M's", and pretty much everything else in the universe, because money makes the world go 'round.

You know what they say: It takes money to make money... or in this case, it's going to take money to host the kind of focus group that's going to help you attract focus group participants. That said, you are going to have to commit to spending money if you want this to work. *So, if you don't have the money...*

...Get the money:

- o Find a funder.
- o Dig into your Funny Money Fund.
- o Have a fundraiser.
- o Look under the mattress...

...Just get the money. Period.

Because a bag of pretzels and can of Diet Coke isn't going

to cut it. You need to be ready to roll out the red carpet, wine them, dine them, give them gift cards or even cash to participate. It might cost you $50-$75 a person.

Think about it… how much have you been pouring into ads and brochures and new member/participant recruitment events? Probably a lot more than a high-level focus group costs to host. And how have those things been working for you?

I'm guessing if they were you wouldn't be reading this book. So, isn't it time you put your money where your intended target audience's mouths are, so you can hear what they have to say?

Because if you're going to bring about the kind of change that will help you thrive, not die, you have to decide it's worth it… that it's worth more than almost anything else you're spending money on right now?

I'm just saying!

Here's what Bernie, Congregation Everytown's President, had to say when I broke the news to him that we needed to conduct focus groups at a trendy restaurant and actually pay for everyone's food and drink (one per person on us… after all sober responses are a lot more reliable!) and (cringe) give them each a $25 Visa gift card to boot:

"That's crazy! We don't have that kind of money. We can't afford it!"

Of course, I said what you think I said. I told him they

couldn't afford NOT to do it. I also reminded him why they hired me. I had already warned Bernie and his board that I wouldn't be going the conventional route. I gave them a heads up that it was going to cost money to do this right. They agreed wholeheartedly… at the time.

But now, cold hard reality had set in. I understood where they were coming from. I really do. It's pretty much everyone's first reaction. But "change or die" and all that… I stayed true to my convictions. It took a few minutes (okay, an hour) to talk him down off the ceiling because -

Change is hard.
Change is scary.
Change threatens the status quo.

Bernie and company decided to rip off the Band-Aid and give it a go. They decided it was worth doing and look what happened! So, what's it worth to your organization to get game-changing information, feedback and ideas?

I get it's easier said than done to take this leap. But leap you must if you want results you can use. Your organization is no different from any other organization in the world. In fact, Jewish organizations are just like people–

o They pick.
o They choose.
o They prioritize.

Every organization needs to decide how to allocate its resources… how to spend its time, talent, energy and money. So, in the future when you're tempted to say to yourself, or when others say (and they inevitably will): "we don't have the money for that," don't let it stop you. At the risk of sounding cliché… when it comes to something that is sure to set you on the path to success, you can't afford NOT to do it!

CHAPTER TEN

M is for Method

You've put together your focus group wish list, made up of people who have a similar level of engagement, age range, gender, or whatever it is that's relevant to who you're trying to reach.

You've asked a few people, representative of the group you want to reach, what it would take to get them to come to a focus group hosted by an organization they weren't affiliated with or that they didn't care much about.

You've gotten the resources (translation: $s) necessary to do it right.

You've reserved your venue and secured a PRIVATE ROOM *(not just a table in the corner, but an entire private room)* because you know how important it is that people can speak freely and hear and see each other. You've been assured that you can get round tables, or have rectangular tables arranged in a large square to invite conversation. You have gone over other details related to food and drink and event management.

Kudos for thinking of all of this in advance!

You've crafted a compelling email or invitation and did all the necessary follow-up to ensure the right number and mix of people will be there. ***You did your best*** to find people to invite who are considered influencers, "cool" or "popular" people with whom others want to associate.

You've also thought to send a confirmation email once they agree to participate (thanking them profusely of course!) You have already written a reminder email that you will send the day before the focus group saying how much you're looking forward to seeing them tomorrow evening with a recap of time, place and other details such as parking, etc. (This will save you from several empty seats that often are a result of people simply forgetting).

That's so smart!

You've secured a note-taker(s) so you can be free to facilitate the group without being incumbered and arranged for all recording equipment if applicable. (Please note, if you are taping the conversation you ***must*** get consent from all members of the group in advance.). Realize that some participants may feel uncomfortable being taped so it can be a little tricky and may incumber some.

Wow! You've thought of everything! So far, so good. Now what? I'm going to tell you... but first, a word about my unscientific approach:

It's unscientific. Or better said, **it's an "unscientific science."**

I completely own that. So please, no cards or letters, snippy emails or nasty reviews telling me this isn't how it's supposed to be done. I get that some organizations and big corporations hire professionals whose only job is to run focus groups. I get that two-way mirrors are often involved and no one from the actual business or organization is supposed to be in the room. I get it...

...but here's what I get even more –

You're not selling athletic shoes or baby strollers or breath mints --

You're selling engagement, belonging and a sense of connection to Judaism/the Jewish people/Jewish life.

Then there's this: By the very fact that you've successfully gotten weakly connected and/or unengaged people from your primo target audience to come to your focus group, *it immediately becomes SO MUCH MORE than a focus group.*

It becomes an intimate *event* where people who probably don't know each other have the chance to get to know each other. And they will get to know each other because their comments and input and participation in this kind of conversation will reveal certain things about them that will likely help them get to know each other a lot more than if they were standing at a crowded bar over drinks and appetizers.

Stay with me here!

If you've done a good job of identifying a great venue and creating a relaxed, safe and friendly atmosphere, chances are good some of these people will make a connection with each other, and maybe even with you and any staff (or committee or board members who promise to listen and not interfere) that you brought with you!

By giving their opinions, suggestions and feedback about your organization - the one with which they are weakly or not at all engaged - they will naturally become engaged, hopefully with each other and with your organization.

I already told you that my 4M formula is an unscientific science…

…but what I didn't tell you is that the science I was referring to is *"Social Science."* Here's the thing:

The focus group event itself can be used as an important method toward building meaningful relationships amongst the participants and with your organization.

So, you **CANNOT** let this opportunity slip through your fingers. Do you see how you get double bonus miles here? *You get solid data from your target audience, and, you get to take your very first step in engaging a population*

83

of people you never would have gotten in front of otherwise.

So... don't blow it.

Seriously, don't blow it. Because this could serve as your jumping off point, your ticket on the express train... your *Fast Pass* to actually attracting the very audience you set out to attract. Please indulge me as I take you on a detour to bring this to a head –

Case in Point #4:

Less than six months into my new job at The Mayerson Foundation, I called together my very first focus group. Our Jewish community was hemorrhaging young adults. They went off to college and never returned, or if they came for jobs at Procter and Gamble, General Electric or other mega companies headquartered in town, they hightailed it out of town as soon as they could get transferred. Something had to be done.

My initial landscape assessment revealed that 95% of Jewish college grads weren't returning home. Of the remaining 5% who did return, the majority said it was merely a stopgap measure until they could save enough money to move to Chicago, New York, Boston, Atlanta or other parts unknown.

Our Jewish community, once a thriving center of Jewish life in America, was at risk of dying a rapid and painful death. It had become a YP (young professional) wasteland.

Something had to be done, but community resources were limited. As a result, I recommended to my Trustees that we step in and use our resources to try and reverse this trend. It became a top priority for our foundation and continued to be throughout my tenure.

After doing lots of homework, I discovered three Jewish twenty-something guys who were known for actually walking up to other young people who they thought might be Jewish - in bars, restaurants and even grocery stores - and inviting them to happy hours they would host at one of their small apartments. These three guys had chutzpah to spare. **Respect!**

I invited them out to the trendiest beer and pizza place in town and asked them to help my foundation put together a focus group of people just like them. Later I learned they only came for the free pizza and beer. I made a mental **"note to self"**: *Keep doing this. It works!* (Turns out that $75 was the BEST money ever spent!).

At first, they were skeptical. Why should they help us? Why did we care so much? No one else seemed to. After all, they had gone to Jewish organizations and agencies asking them to sponsor events, but their requests always fell on deaf ears.

But okay, it was a different time. Ours, like many communities hadn't yet seen the value and critical importance of attracting and retaining this audience. It just wasn't on the top of their priority list yet. As a result, these three twenty-something guys tried to take matters into their own hands. But it was hard to work full-time and try to host happy hours in their tiny apartments with the limited resources that they had.

So, they figured, what could it hurt? They decided to hear me out.

I told them that my Foundation shared the same concerns they did… we thought our community could and should do better by their demographic… that we wanted to support their efforts and would do whatever we could to help make our city a viable destination for Jewish YPs.

I said if they could help me pull together some people for a focus group, I'd treat them all to dinner in a cool venue of their choosing and just talk with them about what they wanted. And if all the stars aligned, I might just be able to give them what they wanted.

As for them, that sealed the deal. We all know that old story about a guy who's granted three wishes. In this case, a major foundation fell from the sky to grant three guys one really big wish. As for me… I found my Sherpas. It was time to start climbing the mountain. They were my target audience, and they were my connection to a lot more just like them. I let them lead the way!

They say that every great journey starts with a single step. So I took it.

I set up a focus group and did all the things I told you to do:

Right mix of people – Check.

Popular venue with the demographic in question – Check.

Perfect set-up for comfortable conversation – Check.

Dinner, a drink and great discussion – Check, check and check.

Nineteen young Jewish adults in their twenties and early thirties agreed to attend. (As I expected, most came for the free sushi.) There was time to schmooze, have a drink, and settle into two groups, which my assistant and I facilitated. We asked them what they wanted… what they needed… what was missing for young professionals in our city.

Most of them weren't affiliated with anything Jewish, and a lot of them didn't know each other when they got there that night.

But guess what?

A few of them actually ended up marrying someone they met at that very focus group, or someone else they met at one of the future events they would go to. Some of them became lifelong friends and stood up at each other's weddings, came to each other's baby showers and enrolled their kids in Jewish preschool together. Some of them went on to hold board positions in the Jewish community such as Treasurer of the Jewish Community Day School, Membership Chair of a Temple, or sit on an Allocation's committees at the Jewish Federation.

These nineteen people were the spark that reignited an entire Jewish community. Their ideas, feedback and input led to the start of one of our foundation's first operating initiatives, Access for Jewish Young Professionals.

Nineteen people turned into 45 a few months later… which turned into 85, then 150… We kept asking, and they told us. We succeeded, we failed, we refined, and we course corrected. We learned, and we grew… and grew…and grew. Hundreds turned to thousands who participated in our programs and events over the years, and today, our city boasts one of the strongest, most vibrant populations of Jewish YPs in the entire region, and in a lot of cases, in cities twice the size. And here's why…

Because we simply asked them what they wanted.

We heard what they had to say.

Then we did everything we could to give them what they asked for.

And because they were a group of similar people who had been brought together for a common purpose, they made connections with each other that they chose to make again and again. It worked because we gave them what they asked for.

It's as simple—and as complicated—as that.

CHAPTER ELEVEN

Hear What They Have to Say

Alright... It's Focus Group time! If a tree falls in the focus group and no one's listening, does anyone hear what is being said?

The answer is NO. I know because I've witnessed focus group situations where Giant Redwood-sized ideas, themes and messages were literally being felled, right into the middle of the room, and the facilitator was completely oblivious.

But I understand. Facilitating a focus group can be tricky, especially if you are intent on getting it right and hope to leave with some actionable ideas and a better, more authentic understanding of your target audience. **Doing it "right" requires a lot more than just asking a bunch of standard issue questions and writing down the answers.** Even the most well-intentioned facilitator can get caught in one of several traps that can threaten to derail

90

even the best laid plans and goals. And speaking of traps, this seems like the perfect time for another…

… Word from our sponsor!

…Now, from the makers of **Trap Tracker,** comes another ingenious early warning system, sure to be every focus group facilitator's best friend. Introducing the **Self-Sabotage Stopper!** a tiny little sensor that's shockingly simple, but surprisingly effective, in curtailing the purposeful or accidental actions of your own worst enemy… **YOU!**

It's easy, discreet and guaranteed to save you from yourself. Listen to what these satisfied facilitators have to say:

Jeremy Schoenfeld, Program Director-

I was a *"Half Listener."* I just needed some warm bodies in a room to confirm what I thought I already knew, so I basically tuned out when the participants started talking. My programs seemed to always end up failing though, until someone told me about *Self-Sabotage Stopper!*

It's a tiny sensor you stick behind your ear. The second it senses that you're tuning out, it tunes you right back in by delivering a low voltage shock down the back of your neck. Now I'm *all in* every time and I learned that actually listening to what people have to say makes a world of difference. My programs are the talk of the town now!

Eve Bernstein, Youth and Family Director-

I used to be a *"Shoot it Downer"*. No matter what the idea, I'd respond with "We already tried that," and "That never works," or "The board will never go for that..." or the ever popular "We can't afford that!" I'd leave the focus groups feeling like no one ever had a doable idea... but then, I heard about *Self-Sabotage Stopper!*

I figured it was worth a try and boy am I glad I did! Now, every time I start to shoot something down, I get a little shock that motivates me to put a positive spin on every response. So instead of saying "that won't work," I now ask, "how can we make that work." Instead of saying "we can't afford that," I now say, "how can we get creative and find a way to pay for that idea?" Shockingly, the participants help problem solve every time. I found that when they're bought in, so much more is possible. I went from being a Shoot it Downer to a Pump it Upper! Thanks *Self-Sabotage Stopper!*

Theo Straus, Special Projects Manager-

I was your classic *"Yes But-er."* I'd always say how I wanted the group to be honest and how I valued their feedback even if it wasn't positive. But here's a little secret, I wasn't being honest with them or myself. I mean, it's true what they say: "the truth hurts." I used to be all about excuses... *"Yes, but* the reason no one came to that event was because it was raining," or *"Yes, but* we didn't know/think/anticipate/expect that to happen." And of course, there was always the *"Yes, but* it wasn't our fault" defense. But when someone said: "It doesn't really seem like you're as open to criticism as you said you would be," I knew I needed help. That's when I turned to *Self-Sabotage Stopper!* That's when everything changed for the better.

Now, the second I start to get defensive; I get a little jolt that reminds me that embracing the feedback will set me free! And lo and behold, as soon as I stopped making excuses, refrained from cutting people off and let them give it to me straight, I actually heard what they had to say. And believe it or not, nothing they said was that hard to do or to fix! Now we've got more people than ever attending our programs. Go figure! I don't know where I would be without *Self-Sabotage Stopper!*

So, if you, or a focus group facilitator you know, could benefit from a little low voltage reminder at your next focus group, pick up a *Self-Sabotage Stopper!* sensor today and open your ears and mind to a whole new world of input and ideas!

Get a little shock before you start to talk and experience the *Self-Sabotage Stopper!* difference for yourself today!

So, what have we learned? If you want actionable, game changing results from a focus group, listen! Really listen so you can HEAR what they're saying. Don't just pretend to hear what they're saying. <u>Don't just hear what YOU want to hear.</u> Really and truly HEAR what they're saying. I can't say it enough.

But don't stop there. You also need to probe further whenever you detect a possible hidden vein of gold, and mine it for all it's worth. You need to ask follow-up questions, explore all responses thoroughly, and delve deeper to bring revolutionary ideas out into the open.

The goal in conducting a focus group is to "know your audience" and "give them what they ask for." But first, you have to understand what they want. Sometimes they don't even know themselves. That's why it's up to you to mine the conversation for those little nuggets that could very possibly turn into pure gold.

The key is to go in with a good idea of what you want to learn. Crafting a list of questions to refer to is smart. However, don't get so caught up in getting through the questions that you miss all that potential gold lying just beneath the surface.

Case in Point #5

Focus groups worked so well for me that I conducted one at least every other month with various target audiences. Not only did these focus groups serve to engage a new population of people who had seldom or ever come to any of our programs, they always yielded idea-rich results and helped keep me up to date with where my target audiences' heads were.

For example, once, while reviewing our tracking data, I noticed a drop off in attendance at some of the holiday-related events we offered for Jewish twenty- and thirty-somethings. I could have ignored this data, chalking it up to whatever convenient excuse allowed me to live in denial. But I didn't. Instead, I took it to my team so we could analyze what the data might be trying to tell us, and we concluded the following: you can change the theme of your young professional Purim party, or other holiday events every year for ten years, but there's a point at which it becomes clear that your audience is ready for something completely new and different.

Okay... we identified what was *likely* the problem, But, what was the solution?

To find out, I asked a focus group about their favorite holiday memory. Even those who grew up with little or no Judaism, or Jewish connection, cited holidays like Passover, Hanukkah, Shabbat at home and at camp, and yes, even Christmas – **#wakeuptothereality!**

Allie: I loved Passover at my grandparents' house. The Seder was long, but I didn't care because I got to help my grandmother make the matzo balls and I was so proud when we served them to the guests. They were delicious if I do say so myself! Even though I don't go to a Seder anymore, I still make matzo balls on Passover and it brings back the best memories!

Tyler: Shabbat at camp was really awesome. We didn't have Shabbat dinner at home, so it felt really special and cool. I loved the singing and dancing and the massive celebration that went on for hours every Friday night. Each bunk got to braid the challah dough after lunch on Fridays. I could smell it baking all over camp. After prayers we would grab big hunks and stuff our faces with it. This kid, Brad could fit like half the loaf in his mouth. It was so good! What is it about that stuff?

Rachel: My family celebrated Christmas and Hanukkah. Sure, opening presents under the tree was great. But honestly, I have far fonder memories of our Hanukkah celebration. It's probably because it involved this whole experience for eight nights. I mean, even when I was in high school and we all had busy lives and activities, the rule was you had to have dinner with the family all eight nights if you wanted to open presents. This usually included potato pancakes the first night or two, and some of our other favorites. After dinner we'd light the candles and then, one by one, everyone got the chance to open a gift. Funny thing is, I don't remember the gifts, but I do remember the dinners. It was a fun time!

After several more stories just like those, I began to see it, clear as day… it was there, right in front of my face… the common theme… the big idea. The thing that was going to take our holiday programming to the next level. Do you see it? If not, look again.

What stands out in every one of the anecdotes? What's the star of every one of their go-to memories? Can you see it now?

FOOD!

That's right… food glorious food. But more specifically, Jewish food. Jewish meals. Jewish memories. Eureka!!!

I followed my gut and quickly changed course with the questioning:

Me: So about eight of you just shared your favorite holiday memory and I can see why those experiences stuck with you. But I couldn't help but notice that every one of your memories centered around food (laughter all around!). Why do you think that was?

Jonah: Tastes and smells stick with us forever. Maybe eating the food or the meal with special people in our lives made everything more meaningful.

Rachel: Hmm! I guess you could say that in some ways, eating "Jewish" food is my connection to my Jewish side.

Jana: I think you're right. I mean there's hamentaschen, challah, matzo with butter (unanimous "yums" all around!) corned beef on rye, kugel and of course, bagels and lox! Oh… and my mom's awesome charoset on Passover! It's all part of Jewish culture, tradition and family… our shared history.

And so on, and so on, and so on…

I scrapped the rest of my prepared questions and followed that thread for the rest of the night. And guess what? That's the night that our most popular, ongoing program for Jewish young professionals was conceived:

I Dare Ya!

JGourmet!

Yep! Interactive Jewish cooking classes. It became clear to me that night that it was the food, and/or the preparation of the food and meal, that stood out in their memories. It evoked warm, loving and happy thoughts that connected them to their Jewish identity.

If that was the case, wouldn't the best way to Jewish twenty- and thirty-somethings' hearts and souls, be through their stomachs?

Had I not been listening... really, really listening, so I could HEAR what they were really saying, I might have missed that. Had I just been phoning in the list of prepared questions; I might have moved right on to the next one without ever having panned for the gold.

Turns out, our JGourmet cooking series filled up in mere hours after it was announced and there was always a waiting list, even after many years. It offered a great way for Jewish young professionals to socialize, while engaging in something fun and interactive that focused on Jewish culture and tradition.

Classes always ended with eating and learning a little more about the holiday we were showcasing. But it didn't stop there. **By working side by side, by enjoying a meaningful, hands-on experience together, deep friendships were formed** and often groups would get together to put on their own potluck Shabbat dinners and celebrate other Jewish holidays at each other's homes.

Some even married each other, and later attended our "Love and Knish's" family cooking classes with their children. (After all, the cooking classes worked with the young professionals! Another focus group for young parents proved it would work for their demographic too!).

And it was all a result of just asking…

… and reading between the lines… and following the thread… and asking more questions, and did I mention, listening, and more importantly, **hearing**.

So, to recap…

Asking is really important.
Listening is really important.
HEARING is critical!

I hope you're hearing me here! *The difference between listening and hearing is huge*, so as the facilitator, you have to keep your brain firing on all cylinders. You have to stay alert, **tease out the hidden nuggets, and be ready to change course on a dime. Hearing** enables you to tune into the nuances and follow the threads that could turn out to be solid gold!

CHAPTER TWELVE

Some Hints for How to Get It Right

You've gotten there early, checked in with the manager, made sure the table has been set up correctly and the wait staff knows what's what. If you have more than 12 people you should get another facilitator and split the group up after initial introductions in order to have a more meaningful, robust conversation with the Focus Groupers.

You've requested they turn off the music in the room when it's time for the focus group discussion to begin, and you've taken a deep breath. You're doing great! People start to arrive. You greet them warmly and try not to let there be too much of an awkward silence… because there will be, at least at first. Prepare to make some small talk that will promote conversation as people come in.

Once everyone is seated, start with an ice breaker. Not

some silly game where they have to guess the word you taped to their back. It's about getting the participants to connect with one or more people in the room if at all possible. You can come up with something, or feel free to use my go-to, never fail ice breaker:

"Let's go around the table. Tell us your name, what you do, and what you think is the best kept secret in town."

Young parents will almost always talk about new places to take the kids. YPs might talk about a little hideout bar or meet-up puppy play group. Baby Boomers might mention an off the beaten path hiking trail or unsung museum. Regardless, it's easy for most people to instantly answer and this prompt usually teases out immediate commonalities amongst the participants and provides great fodder for their future conversations with one another.

You should be the first to answer your own question so you can set the tone and the time frame. It should be less than a minute per person. You have a lot to get to.

Now that everyone has shared and chuckled and sized each other up, it's time to dig in. Start by thanking them for coming. Sorry I know you know that, but some other readers may not! Tell them the reason you invited them. It might sound something like this:

Recently, we looked around and realized that we didn't have enough people like you coming to our programs/services/fill in the blank. We started to wonder why that was. We had some theories, we even started to come up with some of our own ideas for how to get more people like you to come. But we realized that the best people to tell us what we needed to do were the very people we were trying to reach. So that's why you're here. We really just want to hear what you have to say.

Then assure them of all the things you probably already know you should assure them of:

o This is a safe and confidential space.
o We want you to be honest because it's the only way we're going to succeed. So... bring it on!
o There are no bad ideas or suggestions.
o There are no expectations that you will join or contribute to our organization or participate in future programs or events.

And finally, and *very importantly*:

We will do everything we can to make changes and try new things based on the feedback and ideas that get the most traction in the discussion today. However, even the best ideas can present challenges, some small, and some significant. So, while that may mean we have to make some compromises or find creative workarounds, we are committed to finding a way to make it work!
So... let's hear what you have to say...

Time for the first question -

Don't forget, you are dealing with a group of people who don't live in the Bubblesphere. So, try to keep the first question broad so you can work your way into something more specific as their comfort level increases. A lot will depend upon what you're ultimately trying to find out. However, I've found the question I posed in the last chapter, *"What's your favorite holiday memory?"* is usually a great one with which to start and can lead in lots of different directions. You might also consider the following:

o From your earliest memory until now, what was the best party or special event you've ever been to?

o What are you still looking to learn or know or discover?

o Name a time when you felt truly welcomed and included.

But remember:

Don't be a "Yes But-er"…
…a "Half Listener"…
… or a "Shoot it Downer".

Bottom line… **DON'T BE A BUBBLE PERSON!**
And, as you work to move the conversation to a deeper place, remember *Pam's 100% Reliable "Read the Room" Rule.* Ready? Here it is –

READ THE ROOM.

Look at body language and facial expressions. Listen for obvious and not so obvious signs and signals. Pay attention, not just to what they're saying, but what they're doing. How they are acting and reacting.

If the conversation is weak, if your questions aren't garnering ideas, feedback or insight you can work with or use… move on. Ask different questions and/or go down a new path.

If you've got a participant(s) who can't read the room themselves (translation: they won't shut up and give anyone else a chance to talk) … jump in and call on someone else. You might gently say something like, *"Jenna, it looked like you were going to say something. Did you want to comment?"*

If participants start getting animated/excited/engaged about a particular question, or topic of conversation let them stay with it and see where it goes. Remember:

o **Don't limit their thinking by throwing out your own ideas in the beginning.** Give the participants time to do some Blue Sky thinking of their own first. Only after they've exhausted all their ideas should you ask for feedback on yours.

o **Don't ask leading questions.** For example: "You'd come if we hosted a Hoe Down in our parking lot, wouldn't you?" Or, "$118/person isn't too much to ask for dinner and a Fiddler on the Roof Movie Musical Sing-Along, right?".

o **Don't be defensive. Period.** Even if they say your organization sucks… your programs are a hot mess… or your marketing is a joke. Instead, ask them to elaborate and **just hear them**. Do NOT react, make excuses or be a "Yes But-er" even if it kills you. You might actually be rewarded with a game-changing idea or get the wakeup call that will finally get you to take things to the next level. And remember, you just told them this was a safe, judgement free zone where honesty is valued. Prove it!

Okay, you got this! Just one last note regarding two bits of information you should be sure to get while the gettin's good, so don't forget to ask for the following"

1. The most up-to-date contact information, including phone number and mailing address, because you are going to want to immediately follow up with your participants, perhaps with a personal thank you and an invite to an upcoming program. Then you are going to want to stay in touch with them. In fact, you may even want to ask some of the standouts if they'd like to meet one-on-one for coffee to delve deeper into some of the topics that were discussed. And it is smart to send around a sign-up sheet for anyone who might like to be on an Advisory Committee down the road.

2. If at all possible, ask how they like to get information about upcoming programs and events; social media (be specific) email updates, newsletters, information in the mail and so on. Ask questions like: When was the last time you attended something you saw advertised? Where was it advertised (online, print publication, poster...)? What stood

out about the ad and what was it about the program that made you want to go?

If you can tap into the best, most effective ways to market to them, chances are good that those ways will also be the best, most effective ways to market to other people like them.

So, how's it going so far? Obviously, you're still hanging in there so hopefully you're getting the hang of how this works. Great!

But don't rest on your laurels just yet, because everything I've told you up until now is just the beginning. Because the stakes are about to get raised. Here's where we separate the talkers from the doers, the status quo-ers from the 2.0ers.

Now more than ever, it's time step up to the plate and see what you're made of.

So, what'll it be?

CHAPTER THIRTEEN

Give Them What They Ask For

Put up or shut up.

There. I said it.

I know it sounds harsh, but I need you to understand the seriousness of what I'm saying. If you aren't ready/willing/able to put up, or better said, do everything in your power to give your target audience what they're asking for in good faith, then go back to Chapter One of this book, or better yet, re-read the Warning at the very beginning. Or, maybe just give this book to someone who is serious about their organization's success and survival. For better or for worse, simply identifying your target audience isn't enough.

… Asking what they want isn't enough …

…Hearing what they have to say isn't enough. Because, if you aren't going to do everything you can to

Give them what they ask for...

Then it has been nice knowing you. ***Go back to the Bubblesphere.*** Do not pass GO!

But don't forget that your organization will only have itself to blame when the Bubble bursts. Because asking and not doing is even worse than just not bothering to ask at all.

> **It's a tease...**
> > **a lie...**
> > > **a deception...**

And it won't win you a lot of fans. In fact, it will very likely backfire.

Case in Point #6

(A fictitious tale which represents many real cases I have seen)

Once upon a time, in a land called Everytown, lived a four-term Mayor named Mel.

Mel, along with his team of loyal City Council members, set the policy, oversaw the precincts, doled out the dollars, and kept all the businesses and organizations in Everytown humming along in happy, balanced harmony.

It was a big deal to be on the Everytown City Council. It was populated by a lot of old rich people from families for whom parks, schools, food pantries and other social service programs, recreation centers, and even streets and highways were named.

When a Council member retired or died, it wasn't long before one of his or her children were miraculously appointed to fill the vacancy, ensuring that all the policies, tax breaks and incentives, municipal boundaries and laws were kept intact. This also ensured that people with money would always stay in charge. After all, they knew what was best.

Mayor Mel and his Council cared deeply about Everytown. They made it what it was and were hell-bent on making sure it would never change. And thanks to their tight rein, or better said, tight *reign*… it never did!

But even though Everytown never changed, the wants, needs and expectations of the people who lived there did, including the rich people's offspring who had been tapped to take over. However, their offspring didn't get the memo that they were supposed to stay in Everytown and keep things going the way they had always gone.

Unlike their parents before them, most of the next generation weren't interested in making decisions on the golf course, attending self-congratulatory awards' dinners and rubber stamping the same old-school policies year after year. Instead, they sought collaborative opportunities where they could create, innovate and explore a world of possibilities on their terms. The Everytown Elite just didn't get it. As a result, most of the next generation moved to other cities, and (gasp!) those who hadn't moved away weren't interested in being involved in Everytown's brand of backward politics period. *Uh oh!*

The other residents started to get restless too. Nothing ever changed in Everytown. They craved more and better but were always met with excuses and "yes but-ed" at every turn. Mayor Mel and his posse held all the power. They were frustrated!

Sadly, Everytown started to feel the effects. Over the past decade the rich people who had been in control for so long, were dying off. Because their children had moved to other, more progressive towns, there were fewer and fewer of "their kind" to take their place, buy their real estate and keep their businesses running, much less sit on City Council. And for much the same reason, no new rich people, or any people for that matter, were moving there either!

Home values started to plummet, social services and school funding had to be cut back, and the arts and cultural community no longer had wealthy patrons to keep their programs running. Businesses relocated to more vibrant towns where, unlike Everytown, the population of young people and families was growing by leaps and bounds.

Mayor Mel wasn't going to go down without a fight, so he hired the high-priced consulting firm, Municipal Menders, LLC, to fix everything. They suggested that Everytown sponsor a Town Hall meeting to engage residents and make them feel like their voices mattered, like they could play a role in improving Everytown. So smart!

But that's where it ended, because what they did after that wasn't so smart.

They put out an open call to all Everytown residents to come to a *"Night of 1,000 Ideas"* event at City Hall where big easels and lots of round tables dotted the landscape. At each table sat a City Council member who had been trained by Municipal Menders, LLC to facilitate the conversation at their table:

"If someone starts to say something negative, quickly steer the conversation in a different direction. We can't let this turn into a 'bitchfest'."

"Give them a chance to discuss their ideas but don't be encouraging or suggest that the ideas should or could be carried out. After all, we can only do so much, and we have to manage people's expectations."

"Don't forget, we want people to feel like their voices are being heard so make sure you tell them to stick their Post-its to the wall so the Council can review them at a later date. 'Later date' TBD."

There was a video about the rich history of Everytown, and some speeches by Mayor Mel about how much they wanted and valued the chance to hear from the proletariat. Post-its were sprinkled on top of every table for the *Idea Generation and Inspiration* portion of the program, along with cookies and pitchers of lemonade. To say the least, it was the Everytown Bubblesphere at its best!

A few hundred people showed up.

All came in good faith, with hope in their hearts that the City Council would embrace their ideas and listen to their concerns. They took the bait. After all, they were told that their ideas and feedback would be heard and acted upon by the powers that be to help inform new policies, inspire more innovative programs and lead to better services.

They went all in, getting caught up in the fun and the energy of the evening. They got into intense conversations at their tables with likeminded people who were all trying to help make the community the best it could be.

It really felt like positive change was on its way, or better said, it was *engineered* to feel like it was. Municipal Menders, LLC posted a video montage of the interactions that evening on Everytown's Facebook page with lots of happy pics of Mayor Mel and the Council members posing with the participants. They Tweeted from the event and covered all the social media bases. It was a pretty progressive move for a formerly old school operation. Things were looking up! The townspeople felt hopeful again.

There was also a front-page article in the Everytown Examiner. The headline read: *Hundreds Take Part in Night of 1,000 Ideas!* The article quoted Melanie Megabucks, City Council Rep, who said the responses from the evening revealed the need for more services for Everytown's aging population. She went on to say that new school buses and more efficient trash collection would also be a priority going forward.

Wow! How great was that?

But wait... no one mentioned Ron's idea for planting a community garden to enable the food pantry's clientele to have fresh produce...

...or Sarah's call for appointing City Council members who better reflected Everytown's diverse population and socio-economic status...

...or Sandy's feedback that seniors are no longer interested in sitting with150 people in a big multipurpose room at the Everytown Senior Center and eating those rubber chicken and rice "meals" ...

...or Ben and Lindsey's suggestion that they provide incentives for first-time home buyers and better childcare options for working parents...

...and so on and so on and so on.

Neither Mayor Mel nor Melanie Megabucks, or any of the other powers the be mentioned those things then, and even after two years had passed, they still hadn't mentioned, or acted on them -- or the hundreds of other ideas and input, suggestions and feedback that had come out of that the meeting that night.

They thought that just by putting on a show and giving people a voice, the residents would somehow feel empowered. The Everytown elite didn't think they needed to really listen, and certainly, they didn't think they'd have to actually follow through with anything more than some token programs that were mostly smoke and mirrors…

… They didn't think! Period.

At first, they were able to bask in the residual effects of a feel-good night that engaged a ton of people. But, after six months, people started to wonder what had come of some of their ideas. Mayor Mel was at the ready with a great delay tactic:

The event was so great, and so many great ideas came out of it that we're forming committees to start looking into where we're going to go from here so stay tuned… we'll let you know.

Six months after that, when people started to wonder what had ever come of those committees that Mayor Mel was in the process of forming, he again was at the ready with another excuse:

Our City Manager was in charge of putting those committees together, but he recently left to run Othertown's Power Plant. So, once we are able to replace him and bring the new hire up to speed, we'll put that right back on the front burner.

Two years passed, and people stopped asking because the cold, hard realization finally set in. Mayor Mel and his buddies had never really intended to follow through with any of the ideas that came out of the evening. Their real intention was to make people feel like they could make a difference; be the change. Instead, what they really gave them was a first-class ticket on the Lip Service Express – Destination: No Wheresville.

Mayor Mel and Company thought no one would notice. They were banking on the "feel good" to seep into the zeitgeist so new people would come, old people would stay, and everything would get back to normal in Everytown! They figured if they held things off long enough, people would forget, or at least forgive them for their many other priorities getting in the way of progress. And for a while, it worked…

But, judging by the mass exodus of residents and businesses it was becoming clear to everyone that it had all been just a

Tease,

A lie,

A deception.

Because nothing had changed. Mayor Mel and the City Council said they cared. They asked the community to come. They said they'd listen. They promised they'd respond. But when nothing had been done to give them what they asked for, it sent a message so loud and clear it couldn't be ignored.

It somehow felt even worse because they had given of their time and their heartfelt feedback, ideas and input. After all, it had worked. They *did* feel more engaged. They *did* feel like they had a stake in the outcomes. They *did* feel more invested and hopeful and valued.

But after two years of not really seeing any return on their investment, not feeling valued for their time and heartfelt feedback, ideas and input, it just felt bad. Really bad.

As a result, Everytown began to feel the strain in a much more profound way. Not only did they fail in attracting young people and families, they shot themselves in the proverbial foot by underestimating their best hope for a comeback. More and more buildings were boarded up, going out of business sales abounded and even though the student body had significantly diminished, and Everytown's national school ranking had hit an all-time low, their brand-new school buses were the envy of every other town in the region! At least something good came out of the focus group.

With no one left to wear rose colored glasses, the outlook for Everytown became far from rosy!

So, what's the moral of the story?

Mel and his minions learned it the hard way... You can rule the roost and control the pecking order, but if you don't engage the rest of the flock and give them what they want and need, eventually they're going to cry foul and fly the coup. In the end, you'll be left with egg on your face. So…

… If you ask people what they want, you need to give them more than mere chicken feed. And, if you're not ready to give them what they ask for – don't ask. But be warned, if you never ask, the chickens are bound to come home to roost!

I guess Mayor Mel didn't get the memo. But I'm going to give it to you so you can avoid his folly.

MEMO

To: Every organization on the planet
From Those who've learned the hard way
Date: Every minute of every day
Re: Changes to previous audience engagement protocols

It was previously thought that our target audiences would swallow whatever we tried to feed them, that they wouldn't notice if we asked them for their input, feedback and ideas but never really did anything about it. However, we have recently discovered that they're a lot smarter than we gave them credit for. What's more, they deserve better. As such, please note the following change, effective immediately:

- o If you ask them what they want, do NOT pretend you're going to do something about it.
- o Instead, do everything possible to give them what they ask for.

If you have any questions about this, you shouldn't be working here.

Thank you,
The Management

So, what have we learned from this cautionary tale?

If you go to the trouble to ask them, and they go to the trouble to tell you… go the extra mile and actually do what you told them you'd do…

…GIVE THEM WHAT THEY ASK FOR!

Because asking and not doing, is worse than not bothering to ask in the first place. Okay, you get it. But you're thinking, "What if we can't give them what they're asking for?" Drum roll please…

CHAPTER FOURTEEN

Oops There Goes Another Rubber Tree

…You CAN! You'll find a way. If that Ant could move that rubber tree, so can you!

Because in the immortal words of Theodor Herzl, "If you will it, it is no dream."

That's right. **You can almost always give them what they ask for because they almost always ask for things that are reasonable, doable and relatively easy.** Really! After two decades of doing the asking, I never once ran into a situation where I couldn't deliver to some degree. But before I give you examples, I need to issue an obvious disclaimer:

DISCLAIMER –

This isn't about granting every wish or making sure every request or idea comes to fruition. No one expects that. And don't forget what you already told them… the thing I told you to tell them in Chapter 12… the thing you are supposed to make absolutely sure to say:

We will do everything we can to make changes and try new things based on the feedback and ideas that get the most traction in the discussion today. However, even the best ideas can present challenges, both small and significant. So, while that may mean we have to make some compromises or find creative workarounds, we are committed to finding a way to make it work!

So, once you've digested the conversation and mined your memory, debriefed with staff and colleagues who were in attendance, referred back to the notes and listened again to the tape recordings (if applicable) for the nuggets that incited the most conversation, excitement and energy at the focus group… it's time to get to work.

And it will take some work -- and almost always, some creativity -- but it will pay off…

…Because every word in this book has led to this point…
The point of no return:

> …Because you can't turn back - not now…
>> …because the Bubblesphere is already really

overcrowded,

> ...and because you've done every-
> thing you're supposed to do.

Right?

You've changed your own way of thinking. And, of course, you've made a case to the powers-that-be that in order to stay in the game, you're all going to have to keep an open mind to HEAR what your target audience says and commit to making change based on their feedback.

So, don't let anything stop you, including the fear that you can't give them what they ask for. Because you can. I promise. I mean, no one's going to ask for a check for a million dollars, or a chance to meet the Dalai Lama, or request that you offer a lunch buffet on Yom Kippur. If that's the case, they certainly aren't taking the whole thing seriously and should be politely escorted to the nearest exit.

For the most part, you're going to find that people really do want to help you. They are usually realistic, reasonable and willing to compromise in order to move things in the right direction.

Even if someone does suggest something that's too far out of the range of possibility because you don't think you have the resources to make it happen, be honest with the group and employ their assistance in coming up with a solution.

Please note, this is by no means suggesting that you resort to being a "Yes But-er" or a "Shoot it Downer" or get defensive or make excuses. Those things will stop a conversation in its tracks. There are lots of ways of achieving a positive and productive outcome.

Here's a great example of how it's done. **Please note,** where it says "Here's what Zach would have said" those anecdotes were taken from a debrief conversation with Zach regarding what was going through his mind at the time while employing this new approach.

Case in Point #7

I had the opportunity to provide coaching services to Zach, who ran the Young Adult arm of his organization. We put together a focus group to help attract young professionals who were considered weakly engaged in Jewish life. Most of the focus group participants had either come to just one of his organization's events and hadn't returned or had never come at all. After a great ice breaker and some broad questions to get the conversation started, he asked if there was something they could be doing better, or differently, that would interest them in attending one of his organization's events.

The following are some excerpts from the conversation that night:

Jana said: You asked us to be honest, so here's the deal. Your marketing says, "Open to *Jewish* Young Adults 25-

40 years old." I get it and all, but I don't want to be at an event where my non-Jewish friends aren't welcome.

What the old Zach would have said: It's not that your non-Jewish friends aren't welcome, it's just that our goal is to get Jewish people to connect. So, if non-Jewish people are there it defeats the purpose. Plus, the powers that be at my organization will never go for it. The funding we have is to help <u>Jewish</u> people do <u>Jewish</u> things with other <u>Jewish</u> people. So, I'm afraid that can't be done.

But Zach had brought along his own personal *Self-Sabotage Stopper!* with him to the focus group (yours truly!) so he was on his best behavior. He promised us both he would resist the urge to be a 'Shoot it Downer.' And while he was nervous about opening up this can of worms, he decided that there was no turning back. He committed to really HEARING what they had to say.

Here's what the new and improved Zach said instead: What do the rest of you think? Does Jana have a point?

Arielle said: I agree with Jana 100%. I moved here a couple of months ago for my job. So far, I've made a few friends at work, and have been hanging out with one of my neighbors who I met at my apartment complex. None of them are Jewish. If I could bring one of them with me, I might feel more comfortable walking into an event.

Jillian said: She's right. Based on what I heard when we all introduced ourselves, a lot of us here tonight are transplants. I only know two Jewish people in town and they're an older couple who are friends with my parents. I'd totally come to one of your events if I could bring a friend with me.

Jered said: I've thought of coming to one of your events, but my girlfriend isn't Jewish. I'm not going to a party that she can't come to.

<u>What Zach admitted the voice in his head said:</u> WOW! Who knew? I've been living in the Bubblesphere for so long it never occurred to me that a Jewish person wouldn't know other Jewish people or have Jewish friends the second they moved to town. And, oh yeah, not every Jewish person has a Jewish significant other. So right, my organization's rules are actually ruling out a lot of people. Good to know!

<u>What the old Zach would have said:</u> Yes, but… what if one of the Jewish people at the event meets one of the non-Jewish people and they (gasp!) get married? Yes, but… what if it ends up that the non-Jewish people take over and pretty soon there's more of them than there are Jewish people? Yes, but even though she said she was open to change; my Executive Director will never go for this kind of change! ARGH! I hear what you're saying, but… no can do people!

<u>Here's what the new and improved Zach said instead:</u> Everything you're saying makes total sense! I want to make this happen, but we're going to have few challenges to get over. So, let's talk about what those look like, and hopefully you will have some ideas for how we can overcome them. I know we can! So, let me give you a sense for what I think some of the nay-sayers might say.

These events are supposed to be for Jewish people who want to meet Jewish people, so if you invite non-Jewish people, our target audience might as well go to the local Pub Crawl.

And others might say

Community dollars are being spent to help Jewish people meet other Jewish people. Including non-Jews is completely contrary to that mission.

Any suggestions for how to respond to those arguments?

Olivia said: I guess I would tell them that right now they only have an average of 20 participants coming to their events. Doing it our way would probably bring 10 times that many Jewish people. Making the event more inclusive sounds worth it to me.

David said: You don't have to blast out an invitation to the whole mainstream universe to start coming to your events. What if instead of saying "Open to *Jewish* young adults, 25-40 years-old," it said, "Open to Jewish young adults *and their friends*, 25-40 years-old." That way it sends an inclusive message to the group you're trying to attract. They'll get it.

What the others said: Sarah and Kevin and Kyle and pretty much everyone else chimed in with approval. They added ideas and suggestions for how to overcome the challenges and agreed to show up if Zach's organization could find a way to welcome their friends.

So, what did Zach do?

He sketched out a plan for an upcoming event that included the language David had suggested on the promotional materials. He took it to his boss and billed it as a "pilot program" based on feedback from his recent focus group of unengaged people from his target population. He reminded said boss that she and other stakeholders in the organization had agreed that they would try to remain open to the ideas and suggestions that came out of it.

As expected, he got some initial pushback, but Zach made the case for ***Change or Die***, and showed her the data and a transcript of the focus group conversation. He pointed out that opening up their programs to non-Jewish friends would inevitably bring in a lot more ***Jewish*** people, which in the end, was the whole idea. He continued to refer to the data, because "data talks" and asked that they at least try it once to see what would happen.

To Zach's relief, his boss agreed to dip a toe into the proverbial waters. Great job, Zach!

So, what happened?

Based on the feedback from the group, Zach planned a Happy Hour in a private area of a popular pub in town. He contacted all the members of the focus group, thanked them again for their feedback, and personally invited them to the event.

Of the 12 people who participated in the focus group, 10 attended the Happy Hour. Turns out Jered brought his girlfriend, and Arielle brought her neighbor. The other eight came on their own, because they now knew some people who were going – the people they had met and connected with at the (drum roll please…) FOCUS GROUP!

Turns out, 45 other people came too. Of those, only four people brought someone who wasn't Jewish, and three of them were significant others of a Jewish person.

Incidentally, the three who brought their non-Jewish significant others had never come to this organization's events before because in the past, they couldn't bring their… significant others.

This time they came because they knew their partners were welcome, too. And get this, one of them brought his 27-year-old Jewish brother, and another one brought her 24-year-old Jewish roommate. Most of the attendees were either new or had only come to one other event in the past.

Turns out, sending the message that non-Jewish friends were welcome might have been enough. Just knowing that they **could** bring someone who wasn't Jewish, or that it wasn't JUST for Jewish people, made the difference to a lot of people.

Turns out, of the 61 people who participated in the Happy Hour, less than 10% were not Jewish.

Turns out, hundreds of non-Jewish people didn't storm the event, demanding free drinks and appetizers. They didn't come bearing engagement rings to woo unsuspecting Jewish singles into interfaith marriages, and Zach's organization didn't compromise its goal of engaging more Jewish young people. In fact, they met their goal and then some...

And guess what?

Not only did the experiment serve to calm the nerves of the stakeholders, to disprove the arguments of the naysayers, and quash the concerns of the core participants, here's what came of it:

Zach's organization deemed the pilot a success and gave him the green light to keep doing it! Zach was sure glad he had his internal **Self-Sabotage Stopper!** sensor turned on at the focus group that night! He realized that really HEARING what people were saying had an enormous impact on his own success!

Arielle stopped bringing her neighbor after the third event because she started showing up with Adam, who she met at the original Happy Hour (P.S., their wedding was the talk of the town!) Mazel Tov Arielle and Adam!

Jillian, so impressed that Zach had delivered on his promise, asked him to coffee to talk about starting a social group for young women so newcomers to town and others would have the chance to make a few girlfriends in the Jewish community. (P.S. Jillian and Zach are now a "thing!")

These days, the all-women's group Arielle proposed gets together for dinner before big events, which gives them a chance to enjoy time together, make new friends, and provides readymade groups with whom to walk into the party. Close social relationships formed out of these groups for many, resulting in lifelong friendships and even marriage. (**#win/win!**)

After two years, Zach's events have gone from an average of 17 people to about 150, of which an average of about 10% or fewer are non-Jews. Participants not only come, they come back. They are making friendships, finding meaningful relationships and getting involved in their Jewish community.

Zach asked his target audience what they wanted. He HEARD what they had to say and then… he gave them what they asked for! This led to a big promotion and a raise! (Not to mention a new girlfriend, and the pride of knowing he had been instrumental in building a vibrant program for Jewish young adults in his community!).

What's the moral of the story? If at first you want to say *no can do*, don't go there! TRY, TRY AND WIN! Because when you figure out a way to give people what they ask for, everyone wins!

CHAPTER FIFTEEN
The Ask, The Give and The Glory

I've run several hundred focus groups in my career and have consulted with many others who have run focus groups. While some ideas are easier to execute than others, most have their share of challenges. It's not the job of your participants to think through all the ins and outs, the pros the cons, the complex political implications, or the dozens of hurdles that could potentially stand between even the most reasonable request and the realization of said request.

Nope. That's *your* job!

And your job is hard.

But you don't need a PhD in Rocket Science. You're already smart and capable and able to think on your feet. That's all it takes. But just by way of example, let me walk you through a few scenarios from past focus groups that I ran in my own role as Director of Jewish Innovation and Engagement, to help illustrate how we managed to "give them what they asked for" or close enough...

A focus group regarding programming for Access, The Mayerson Foundation's initiative for Jewish Young Professionals:

The Ask:

A lot of us aren't always interested in attending events in which the majority of people in the room come from the same cultural background. It would be great if you could offer some programs that include a more diverse population of people from other cultures and walks of life.

The Give:

Did I need to put them all on a plane for a field trip to the UN? No. It was simply a matter of contacting the presidents of the local young professionals' groups in the Hispanic, African American, Muslim and Hindu communities and getting them together with a some of the Jewish young professionals to plan a series of cultural events throughout the year that brought the groups together through fun, social activities.

A fan favorite was the Chrismakwanzakah Party, a celebration of Christmas, Hanukkah and Kwanza in partnership with the Urban League Young Professionals. Each group brought food and activities to share with the others. The Urban League Young Professionals took the trophy in the Dreidel Showdown Tournament, an epic upset for the Jewish young professionals who had been playing the game all their lives! To the victors went the spoils, or in this case, foil covered gelt!

The outcomes that resulted from their input:

These events continued, and always packed the house. They served as a great opportunity for networking and helped build important bridges between these groups, positively effecting relations amongst the future leaders in each of the respective communities. **#givethemwhattheyaskfor.**

A focus group regarding The Mayerson Foundation's initiative, Shalom Family for families in the Jewish community with children 12 and younger:

The Ask:

Every time we go to one of your Shalom Family events there are hundreds of people there. That's fine for families with older kids, but it's overwhelming for toddlers and babies. We want to meet Jewish families in the community, but it's too hard with really young children in that kind of setting.

The Give:

Of course, we asked about the times and days that would be best, and the kinds of things they'd like us to offer, so a quick call to a nearby kiddie gym was all it took. For a small fee, on one Sunday per month, we were able to rent the space, along with one of their staffers, before they opened to the public. We added Melissa, a Jewish pre-school teacher, into the mix, who could sing and play the guitar. We renamed her Miss Meliss, for marketing purposes and limited the group to no more than 40 people comprised of about 16 babies/toddlers and one or both parents per child

After free play and time for schmoozing, Miss Meliss ran a lively fifteen-minute circle time that focused on upcoming Jewish holidays, complete with cute songs and fun props. We threw in a healthy, toddler-friendly snack and some coffee and bagels for the parents, and *Sensory Sunday* playgroups were born.

The outcomes that resulted from their input:

These play groups continued over the years and served as a perfect feeder for the larger Shalom Family events when the kids got older, but also for area Jewish preschools, day schools, camps and congregations. The best part was that many of the families became good friends with one another long after their children were too old to attend the Sensory Sunday program. **#givethemwhattheyaskfor.**

A focus group regarding engaging Jewish young professionals at the JCC in a mid-sized community:

The Ask:

When you walk into the lobby of the JCC all you see are strollers and walkers. If you're not a young parent or a senior citizen, it doesn't seem like this is the place for you. As young adults, we'd rather go to a gym where the classes are populated by people our age, and that are geared toward the things we like to do (Chair Yoga and Zumba are not exactly our thing!) We want to get in a great workout and socialize too, and that's not going to happen for us at the JCC.

The Give:

Did we try to convince the JCC to change their class lineup for a demographic who might or might not show up? Did we sink thousands of dollars into instructors and lots of bells and whistles to incentivize young adults to come? We could have. But it wasn't necessary. We found out what they loved doing and gave them the chance to do it, just bigger and better than before.

One of the athletic apparel stores in the mall ran yoga classes several mornings a week in their shop. We asked them if they could provide an instructor for a one-time event at the JCC. We also talked about other ideas for making this a win/win proposition for both entities.

The outcomes that resulted from their input:

We put on a Supersized Yoga event at the JCC. We reserved the multipurpose room on a Thursday night at 6pm. We promoted Danielle, the athletic apparel store's superstar yoga instructor. We added in a special trunk show with some of the newest yoga fashions and gear and a healthy "Smoothie and Bowl Buffet" for dinner after the workout so participants could hang out and socialize. It was a hit! 110 young people showed up that night. It was wall-to-wall twenty- and thirty-somethings!

That's when the JCC's *"Supersize Workout Series: Exercise and Socialize"* was born. We took the kind of classes that were popular with this demographic and "supersized" them. "Supersized Knockout" run by boxing instructor Joey was a fan favorite for both guys and girls. This series, along with several other strategic programs that resulted from focus grouping the target audience, enabled the JCC to go from a handful of paid members from the Jewish young adult demographic, to more than 400 in not much more than two years. **#givethemwhattheyaskfor.**

A focus group regarding how to increase enrollment of young families in a Jewish Community Day School:

The Ask:

We'd consider enrolling our kids in the Jewish Day School, but they only take children three and older. What about babies and toddlers? With both parents rushing to get out the door for work each morning, it's not practical for us to drop one child off at Jewish preschool and the other off at the daycare center in the opposite direction. Pick up is just as much of a hassle. If the Jewish Day School had a preschool that started as early as six months, we'd be much more inclined to consider it. Otherwise it's just easier to keep all our kids in one convenient location.

The Give:

This one was the trickiest of all. At the time, the Jewish Day School in question only took children three and older. The school was reluctant to find more classroom space, get the licensed teachers and gear up for including young babies in the mix. In short, they weren't keen on having to rethink their entire strategy.

But other than the high cost of a Day School education, no one had ever really considered this additional hardship from the parents' perspective, which they came to find out, had been a huge factor in limiting enrollment. This was powerful feedback worth examining further. So that's what they did.

Instead of immediately jumping the gun they conducted more focus groups, sent out a survey, and met with the other Jewish preschools in the community. This enabled them to work through the politics and get the support of the board and community members to rethink their financial model and strategy. In the end, the Day School couldn't ignore the overwhelming sentiment amongst their target population and decided to compromise by opening their preschool to children 18 months and up. Based on the great results, they are now considering lowering the age to accommodate younger babies.

The outcomes that resulted from their input:
The Day School's preschool is the best feeder to their upper school. Without a strong preschool they are at risk of going out of business. Financial aid doesn't mean much to busy parents who can't make two or three stops to drop off and pick up various children before and after work every day. By lowering the preschool enrollment age, the Day School was able to increase overall enrollment by 33%!

Okay. You get the idea. And yes, there are going to be times when some people in the focus group disagree with others in the group, and you worry you won't be able to please everyone. There'll be times when there are 20 great ideas and it feels overwhelming, and times when there are few or no good ideas and you feel like you're right back where you started. But guess what?

You're smart...
You're capable...
...You can think on your feet!

You've got this! You're going to ask the participants to help you come up with solutions to some of the challenges. For example, one such challenge might be when half the focus group participants want one thing, but the other half want something different. In this case, the facilitator might say: ***By doing what this half of the group suggests, it means the other half won't get what they want. Is there a way make it work for everyone?***

You're going to ask them to help you prioritize the ideas if there are too many to execute all at once. Or, if they're light on ideas and suggestions, come up with some prompts that will start a discussion that will lead you down a more productive path.

You're going to look for common themes, listen for subtle nuances, change course when you need to, toss out your prepared questions when the conversation is getting too good to derail. You're going to nail it. And then you're going to come away with a ton of actionable data that you will use to inform your way forward.

Right? *Right.*

Because from this day forward, you're not going to look back. You're not going to keep doing the same things over and over, expecting different results…You're not going to continue to repeat unsuccessful patterns or hope that outcomes will improve without any changes in strategy…You're not going to allow yourself or others in your organization to live in denial that dwindling participation is just a passing phase.

You're going to take a long hard look in the mirror and do what you need to do to make real and lasting change by:

- o **Striving for excellence.**
- o **Taking calculated risks.**
- o **Learning from your mistakes.**
- o **And holding yourself and your organization accountable (even when no one is looking!).**

You're going to accept the challenge and dare to make change. You're going to go the distance? And you're going to make it out of the Bubblesphere and into a creative and exciting new reality where innovative ideas have a chance to flourish.…

… Where people speak a whole different language

that includes words like "yes" and "can" and "why not."

...Where decisions aren't dictated by money and power but instead, are driven by the consumers themselves.

...Where the future is bright because the leadership holds itself accountable and isn't afraid of change!

I promise that place is real. It really does exist, and I know you can get there. So, put that pedal to the metal, it's time to go give them what they asked for!

CHAPTER SIXTEEN
Taking a Cue from the Classics

Meet Sam. Every morning since he could remember, Sam enjoyed a bagel for breakfast. But Sam started to feel tired and weak and wasn't as productive as he used to be. His doctor suggested he needed a little more protein in his diet, something that would bring back his energy and vitality, make him more productive, and keep his body going. When the doctor told him to try Green Eggs, Sam said:

> I am Sam. Sam I am.
> Green eggs just aren't my jam.
> Bagels get me from here to there.
> So leave me be, I just don't care.

The doctor responded:

> *You can eat them with some lox,*
> *Please just think outside the box.*

I will not eat them with some lox,

I cannot think outside the box.

I warn you, Sir, you'll be in trouble
If you can't burst forth from that Bubble

Annoyed, Sam replied:

If you'll kindly back off, I'll take a bite…
…YUM! These are fantastic – YOU WERE RIGHT!

I am Sam. Sam I am –
Who knew Green Eggs would be my jam!

Making change can be hard to do,
It takes courage to try something new.

So, if you've lost your oomph, but still give a damn,
You'll bounce back to life if you play it like Sam!

Dr. Seuss told you way back in the day (starring a slightly different character who was cool with the whole "ham" thing) way before I told you, that no matter how resistant we are to change, if we embrace it, we might be surprised that it actually can turn out to be "just what the doctor ordered!"

And now that you've committed yourself to trying some Green Eggs yourself by bursting out of the Bubblesphere, you are ready to create a new reality that will allow you to make the kind of change that will bring people in, get them to stick around, and keep them coming back.

And you've committed yourself to going all-in by doing the four things I told you that you need to do. That's right, just four. Bottom line – this whole book was really just about doing four simple things. Yes, there were a lot of words in between, but in the end, it was really about:

1. **Identifying your target audience(s).**
2. **Asking them what they want.**
3. **Hearing what they have to say.**
4. **Giving them what they ask for.**

Period. End of sentence. Dead stop.

Now don't get me wrong. I'm hopeful that all the words in between led you on a journey that allowed you to discover for yourself what you need to do to succeed, and the reasons why. And while we're making comparisons to iconic characters from classic literature, I'd like to point out that Dorothy had to follow the Yellow Brick Road all the way to Oz to realize she had the power the whole time to get where she needed to go. But first, she had to find

The Smarts,
> **the Heart, and of course,**
>> **the Courage.**

And hopefully, you have too!

But before I wish you a heartfelt mazel tov and send you on your way, I'd be remiss if I didn't mention something really, really important.

Here's the deal. You're not out of the woods. Not yet...

Actually, not ever. Sorry to break it to you, but you'll NEVER be out of the woods. Because, by its very nature, change is dynamic. It's the opposite of staying the same. ***Change is like an eternal light that must be kept burning. It's your job to keep it lit.*** And, in order to keep the flame from going out you must constantly be asking and hearing and doing. You must always be…

analyzing, evaluating and reevaluating…

tweaking and fine tuning…

and sometimes, rethinking and redoing…

…and you must be ready to turn on a dime, if after giving it a reasonable amount of time, you see something's not working, or could be working better.

And you can NEVER stop -
Asking what they want,
Hearing what they say, and
Giving them what they ask for.

All of this might mean that you have to host several focus groups every year. **#neverrestonyourlaurels!**

Actually, I hosted at least one a quarter for every initiative I ran, sometimes I held one every other month. When it came to the programs and events we ran, I was always "reading the room," watching for new trends, tracking attendance and analyzing who was coming, as much as who wasn't. But when the data seemed to be telling me to make a change, my gut instinct told me not to just go with my gut. **It told me to always ask my target audience, and never be a Bubble Person.**

I mean I probably could have ridden the wave for a couple of years before it would have caught up with me, before attendance would have fallen off to the point at which I couldn't deny it. I could have saved myself, my staff, and my Foundation a lot of time and money by not continuing to collect data, hold focus groups, and track participation so carefully. But I'm so glad I didn't give into the temptation. Because all of that paid off in such a big way. And it will pay off for you too. Take a deep breath, stick to your convictions, stand up to the skeptics and ignore the naysayers. You have a job to do and your job is hard. It's going to take courage, commitment, perseverance and certain amount of good old-fashioned chutzpah to pull it off.

But you have what it takes…

So get ready…

…get set…

…it's time step out of the Bubblesphere.

Don't forget your sunglasses…

…And there was light!

Exodus

Breaking away from the familiar isn't easy. Even the Israelites had to wander around for quite a while to get it right. But through all the ups and downs, they made it to the Promised Land, and so will you.

Hopefully I've given you some guidelines to follow that will help you on your journey. But remember, all travelers encounter their own unique challenges along the way.

As I mentioned, for nearly 18 years I had the enviable good fortune to be in an environment that fostered Blue Sky Thinking - an environment that allowed me to explore and experiment... to fall down and get back up... to learn and to grow... to challenge and to make change. That is why I've dedicated my life to spreading the strategies and expertise I acquired as far and wide as possible to help reverse the trend of declining Jewish engagement.

I will never take the opportunity I've been given for granted and will always be grateful for the chance it has afforded me to help others who care as deeply as I do, about the future of the Jewish people. It's why I wrote this book, and why I chose to start my company, Be Bold Creative, and become a Jewish Engagement Consultant.

I hope you got a lot out of this book and wish you and your organization the very best success in all your endeavors. Here's to health, happiness and the ability to do important and meaningful work that adds value to people's lives and brings fulfillment to you and all the others who work hard every day to make our world a better place.

So, stay courageous…

> **… be persistent…**

>> **… and more than anything else,**

>>> **remain focused.**

Good luck! Now go out and make that change!

I Dare Ya!

Stay tuned and Stay in touch

What I wrote in these pages is just the tip of the iceberg. Keep on the lookout for my how-to sequel, *I Double Dare Ya!,* which builds on what I covered in this book and takes a deep dive into effective strategies for innovative programming and marketing for Jewish audiences. In the meantime, you can visit my website at **www.beboldcreative.net** for lots of examples you can use. Plus, you can sign up to receive notices for the release of my next book as well as all of my upcoming webinars, speaking engagements, workshops and more.

Special Thanks

With undying gratitude to all my fellow travelers who have accompanied me on this journey... who pumped me up, and also picked me up when I fell down, and who gave me the tools, the courage and the support I needed to reach this meaningful milestone... *Shehecheyanu!*

Trevor Evans • Douglas E. Richards • Sandra Richards • Ronald Richards • Rabbi Seth Bernstein • Marsha Bernstein • Dr. Neal Mayerson • Manuel D. Mayerson, *z"l* • Dr. Donna Mayerson • Rhoda Mayerson • Arlene Mayerson • Breta Cooper • Chris Jenkins • Rabbi Miriam Terlinchamp • Jill Ross • Julie Brook • Pam Harris • Vered Danovich • Lisa Hacker • Julie Pakrosnis • Julie Robenson • Rachel Plowden Kohn • Nikki Sandor • Briana Landesberg Warm • Jordan Edelheit • Matt Steinberg • Rachel Rothstein • Jana Sharp • Tsipora Gottlieb • Adam Rosenberg • Rob Calif • Jeff Harris • Netanel (Ted) Deutsch • Dr. Kristin Patterson

And most of especially... to my husband and children: Sonny, Karly, Kevin and Sarah